NEVER SAY NEVER

NEVER SAY NEVER

The Psychology of
Winning Golf

BOBBY NICHOLS

FLEET
Publishing Corporation · New York

Contents

INTRODUCTION

No golfer is a hopeless case.

Bobby Nichols is living, championship proof of the fact.

After a near fatal automobile accident in 1952, Nichols had to learn to sit up and walk again. The long convalescence gave him time to think.

Nichols had to fight an uphill battle against pain, the dismal outlook of being a cripple and the psychological demoralization that accompanies it. Had it not been for the many bedridden hours he spent with his golf grip alone, Nichols' hands might not have been so sensitive to the proper feel of the clubs.

Had he not lain day after day envisioning the swings of Ben Hogan, Sam Snead and Byron Nelson, imprinting them on his subconscious mind, the smooth golfer might not have developed.

Nichols' accident occurred on the night of September 4, 1952, the day before he was to start football practice at St. Xavier High School in Louisville.

He was in an automobile speeding south on Breckinridge Lane, passing the plush fairways of Big Spring Country Club, where Jim Turnesa had won the National Professional Golfers' Association title.

Bobby had no uneasy premonitions about the curves ahead, even as he watched the driver's foot go down and the speedometer climb to 107 miles an hour. The breeze brought relief from oppressive heat. Anyway, 16-year-olds don't worry. They dream. Bobby was thinking about Turnesa and how nice it was to be a real champion.

Bobby had won the Louisville caddie tournament, so he knew what it was like to be a champion—at least on a small scale.

Thoughts of golf greatness were interrupted. The car wasn't going to make the curve. Bobby braced himself.

It was 8:15 P.M.

By 8:30, a hundred persons were busy trying to extricate four boys and a girl buried beneath twisted steel that had been draped around a telephone pole.

A priest administered the last rites of the Catholic Church to Bobby Nichols.

"Don't worry too much about this one," directed a doctor, pointing to him. "He won't make it. Let's try to save the others."

General Hospital was a scene of confusion that would have outdone the most spectacular television serials. Doctors and nurses hurried about. The tumult was not unusual for the hospital, especially on weekends and holidays, but it created terror in the heart of Bobby's mother, Artie Nichols.

"He's in there," said Owen, her husband, "but I don't think you ought to see him—not yet, anyway."

Artie Nichols glanced into the emergency room. A priest knelt beside a stretcher. She wondered why there were no doctors around the lifeless form and hoped that God would forgive her for wanting it to be somebody other than Bobby.

An hour passed. She looked for any clue to Bobby's condition— the expressions on the faces of nurses, noises from the emergency ward, and the calm voice of the public address system.

While she waited she consoled herself with memories.

She remembered Bobby's first set of golf clubs: *He was ten years old and slapped an iron shot that hit one of his daddy's hens in the head.*

Bobby was terrified at what his father would do to him for killing

the hen. She had asked Bobby how it happened and he replied:
"Well, I told her to move."

A doctor came down the hall and Artie Nichols held her breath.

"I forget to tell you that I had to make a quick incision near the left hand to give him a blood transfusion," said the medic to Owen. "He might never be able to use the hand but it will help if the hand is massaged."

It was two days before all the laboratory reports were in. Bobby had a brain concussion, a broken pelvis, a punctured spine, a collapsed lung, a bruised kidney and "other internal injuries."

"Chances are, he'll never walk again," said the doctor to Owen Nichols. "There will be a change one way or the other in ten days. If he survives that period, his chances of recovery will be good but he may be a cripple the rest of his life."

The next ten days were days of hope and prayer for Owen, Artie and Cathy Nichols, Bobby's older sister. She and her father sat through critical nights hoping for signs of a rally. Bobby mumbled incoherently and tossed and tried to turn but the pain in his broken body wouldn't permit it.

The vigil was a long one. On the 13th day, Bobby suddenly opened his eyes.

"How long have I been asleep? Did I miss football practice?" he asked Cathy. He didn't need an answer. As he tried to get out of bed he could feel the bandages and braces that surrounded his body. Cathy, jubilant, rushed to call her mother and father.

September 18th was a red letter day for Bobby Nichols. He was moved from General Hospital to St. Joseph's Infirmary. It was a true indication that Bobby was improving, even if he might never walk again.

October 8 was another big day. John Meihaus, who would have been Bobby's football coach at St. Xavier's High School, came to take him home.

"You'll be playing golf in no time," said Meihaus as he carried Bobby from the car to his room. Meihaus suppressed his real thoughts.

Owen, Artie and Cathy massaged Bobby's left hand several times every day. It had begun to show signs of life but it was too early to determine whether it could be saved.

Brother Edward Joseph, golf coach at St. Xavier, was a regular visitor at the Nichols home. Bobby had played on the team that had won the Kentucky championship in the spring.

Brother Joseph talked golf. In a way, Artie didn't like this because she knew when he left, Bobby would call for his clubs again. She couldn't bear the sight of him holding golf clubs when he hadn't learned to sit up in bed. Brother Capistran tutored Bobby in his studies.

Early in November, other Xavierian Brothers joined in the rehabilitation of Bobby Nichols. Artie Nichols was glad to see them. They seemed to boost Bobby's morale, which was a big factor now. A 16-year-old who has been so active has difficulty reconciling himself to lying flat on his back. The brothers tried to keep Bobby's mind on his school work and off his apparently hopeless physical condition. Despite their efforts, Bobby's spirit took a nosedive.

"I have an idea that might help," one of the visitors, Brother Jerome, told Bobby's father. "Anyway, we have nothing to lose. The boy doesn't want to get well."

Brother Jerome knew that Bobby idolized Ben Hogan.

In early February of 1949, Hogan's automobile and a bus collided on a Texas highway. Hogan suffered broken bones, complications set in and a blood seepage caused formation of a clot that threatened his life. A month after the accident Hogan underwent a two-hour abdominal operation to correct the condition.

By midsummer, Hogan was hobbling around on crutches. In December, he played his first game of golf. Then, he announced he would attempt a comeback in the Los Angeles Open in January.

Walking stiffly on damaged legs, Hogan amazed the golf world. He finished in a tie with Sam Snead, shooting a remarkable 280. Hogan lost the playoff but he got a big lift in morale. He went on to win the U.S. Open title the next two years.

The brothers decided a letter from the great Hogan would benefit

Bobby more than any medicine. So they wrote Hogan to ask his help.

Bobby liked mail—any kind of mail. When his mother handed him a letter with the return address of Ben Hogan in the upper left hand corner of the envelope, Bobby thought it was a gag.

He tore open the letter and learned that it wasn't.

"I don't know if there is anything I can say to you that would console you mentally or physically since I know you have been through everything," wrote Hogan. "I always figured that no one ever went through life without something happening to them, some of them minor and some major.

"Those of us who have the minor things just don't have to work as hard recuperating as the people like you who have the major things.

"Also, I don't have to tell you that the human body probably is the greatest machine ever known—plus the fact that, given a chance, it will heal any sickness or hurt.

"It is the determination and will of a person to do the exercises that will get him well, and, as you certainly know, there are no shortcuts."

Hogan concluded:

"I don't want to sound like a preacher and hope you understand my thoughts for you. I am terribly sorry for your misfortune and you shall be remembered in my prayers."

When the Xavierian Brothers came to the Nichols home the next night, they were gratified at the result of a few lines of encouragement. They saw a cheerful, bright-eyed chap showing the letter to everybody who came into his room.

Bobby was determined to walk and play golf again.

Little did Nichols or Hogan realize that 12 years later they would be in the same threesome in the Professional Golfers' Association tournament and that the presence of Hogan would inspire Nichols to put the finishing touches on a record 271.

One day, shortly after receiving the letter, a momentous thing happened. Bobby sat up for the first time. It was like a kid learning to ride a bicycle, or a teen-ager getting his driver's license. One big event led to another. Bobby eventually was able to stand up on crutches. "I couldn't get him off of the crutches," Mrs. Nichols recalls. "He was completely fascinated by being able to stand and walk a little." Being upright was different from the way Bobby had been for weeks and he loved it.

Still, Bobby Nichols on crutches was a pathetic sight. Although his mother had massaged them every day for weeks, his legs were all bone from disuse.

Bobby visited Audubon Country Club where he had caddied. The caddies and the pro, Bobby Craigs, looked at him as if he were walking death. It irked Bobby for them to talk of his golf in the past tense, as if he never would play again.

Bobby sometimes wondered himself. His arms ached from hobbling around on crutches but the exercise did them good. Bobby's ambition was to be a golf professional and travel the tour but he knew he was a long way from that goal.

The day Bobby threw his crutches away was one of the happiest of his life. He was still wobbly and had to hold on to things but it was another step of progress—progress against what the doctors said was a hopeless cause.

At first, Bobby could practice putting for brief period, but he couldn't swing a golf club yet. He got tired trying to stand up for putting practice and had to rest frequently.

He wondered about his timing and balance—the qualities that helped him win the caddie tournament. Would the long period of injury and convalescence destroy them?

A week or so after putting aside his crutches, Bobby went to a golf course with a friend, Lee Hasenour, who also attended St. Xavier. Bobby wanted to see if he could hit a golf ball yet.

Lee handed Bobby a driver and teed the ball up for him.

"Go ahead and cut loose, Bobby," said Lee. "You can hit it."

Bobby could hardly stand up, but he took a mighty swing. The ball zoomed down the fairway about 250 yards.

Lee got mad.

"What are you trying to do, pull my leg or something? You knew you could hit the ball. Who are you trying to kid?"

Bobby was plenty tired after that one big swing. It made him wonder if he would ever regain the stamina to play 18 holes.

Three weeks later, he did. At least one ambition was realized. Bobby was playing golf again. He had an 82 and while that might not seem like much of a score, it looked like a sub-par round to Bobby. Improvement was rapid. In June, Bobby shot a 3-under-par 33 on the last nine at Fort Knox to win the Kentucky high school golf title. He had recaptured skill as well as stamina. His left hand, the one which his father had massaged, bothered him occasionally but the feeling that he had regained something that was feared lost offset the hurt.

"They never did tell me how bad I really was," said Nichols, later. "When you stay in bed 74 days, you do a lot of thinking. It made me more serious about life and about golf."

Bobby never had a chance to go out for football at St. Xavier but the school's coach did not desert him. "Johnny Meihaus was at my bedside every time I woke up," said Nichols. "He was there when the hospital released me and he used his car to take me for rides to golf courses while I was getting my sea legs."

When Bobby graduated from St. Xavier, Meihaus got him a scholarship at Texas A. & M. from Paul Bryant, coach and athletic director.

Bobby Nichols was a freak in college. He attended Texas A. & M. on a football scholarship but he never punted or passed or ran and he didn't block or tackle anybody. He played golf. Golf officials frowned on scholarships in those days.

Texas A. & M. Athletic Director Paul Bryant told Johnny Meihaus, the St. Xavier football coach, that he wanted to have a really good golf team and would accept "sixty shooters."

During Nichols' senior year at St. Xavier, Meihaus called Bryant and said: "I got one for you."

It later became obvious that Meihaus hadn't exaggerated. Nichols won the Southwest Conference title during his sophomore year.

It was the biggest tournament he had won up to then and it convinced Bobby that he wanted to make golfing a career.

After the Southwest Conference tournament, Nichols returned to Louisville and won seven of eight tournaments, including the Kentucky Amateur and the Kentucky Public Links.

Henry Ransom, former touring pro and Texas A. & M. golf coach, was one of the biggest influences in Nichols' life. He polished Bobby's game.

At the time, Ransom commented: "Bobby can go as far as he wishes. He has the size and the temperament. About his only weakness is a relative inability to finesse shots from 100 yards on in. As long as he can swing all out, he's all right. But he'll learn this from experience."

While attending Texas A. & M., Bobby's roommate, Marcelino Moreno, took him to Midland, Texas, for a visit.

"I liked Midland, especially the Midland Country Club," said Nichols. "I liked Texas so well that I played amateur golf in the state for the next two summers."

After receiving a degree from Texas A. & M. in business administration, Nichols became assistant pro to Boyd Huff at Midland Country Club.

In 1960, Huff talked a group of Midland businessmen into putting up $10,000 to guarantee Nichols' expenses on the pro tour. Nichols already had played against professionals.

He qualified for the National Open at Tulsa in 1958 and survived the cut at the end of 36 holes. He wound up 50th.

Even though he knew that competitive golf as a living would be touch and go, his heart was set on it. His subsequent career has shown how right he was. Nichols has learned some psychological as well as technical shortcuts during his spectacular career. In this book he passes them on in his own words.

Nichols picks his All-American golf team in the book. For my money, Nichols himself should be on it. He was named putter of the year by the golf writers and medium iron player on Golf Magazine's All-American team.

DEAN EAGLE

Chapter One

GOLF IS A THINKING MAN'S GAME

An $18,000 putt is something that doesn't happen to many golfers.

I had one on the 72nd hole of the Carling Open at Oakland Hills Country Club in Birmingham, Michigan. To make matters worse, a fellow named Arnold Palmer was looking over my shoulder.

There it was, 18 inches from the cup—$1,000 an inch.

If golf were a team sport, this would have been a good place to send in a substitute. But there are no pinchhitters on the pro tour. A man must handle his own dilemmas.

Strangely, I wasn't perturbed by the 51-foot approach putt over a hogback. I feel that I'm going to make every putt, or, at least, get close enough for an easy tap-in.

I studied the 18-inch putt closely but I confess I didn't think of what a miss would cost. I felt that I could make it even if a firecracker were set off on my backswing.

I tapped the ball gently and watched it out of the corner of my eye as it dropped into the cup. I concentrated mainly on keeping

A HAPPY WINNER . . . Louisville's Bobby Nichols dropped his putter and waved his arms after sinking the final putt to win the World Golf Tournament in Birmingham, Mich., by one stroke over Arnold Palmer.

my head still. I knew that if I did this, it was a routine putt.

No special heroics or talent is required to make 18-inch putts. They're automatic. But the mind must be in charge at all times on a golf course. One mental slip and any putt can be fouled up.

There are maybe 50 pros with all the shots needed to win a big tournament. Players who win most of the money are those with the right mental attitudes.

Of the 8,000,000 golfers in the United States, only 1,500 are "scratch" players. Their handicaps are zero. They shoot par regularly and obviously have the right mental attitude and the physical stamina with which to back it up.

The breakdown is something like this:

Players	Handicap
1,500	Zero
68,500	1 to 3
1,903,200	4 to 12
2,806,400	13 to 18
1,945,699	19 to 24
1,275,200	25 and up

Fortunately, the fellowship at the 19th hole is superb and golf is a game in which the handicap is a great leveler. The par shooter or "scratch" player can give the 18 handicapper a stroke a hole and it turns out to be quite a match.

With a few psychological aids, the 36 handicapper can drop to the 20 class and the 20 handicapper can develop into a 10 handicapper. The 10-handicap player occasionally can shoot par.

Inasmuch as all golf movements come from the brain, psychology can be stronger than a well-stroked two iron or a deadly putter because it works on every club, on every shot and on every hole.

3

Get the picture.   *Study but don't fret about bad shot.*

MY 12-POINT APPROACH

Here are twelve psychological props that have helped me—I call them the Mental Dozen. Unfortunately, I had to learn most of them the hard way.

1. GET THE PICTURE

It is important that both budding young golfers and ambitious old ones get the image of a good swing. The correct mental image inspires confidence.

Most golfers, after being out in the open all day, don't have to count sheep to go to sleep. For those who do, I can't think of a better substitute than to drift into dreamland to the accompaniment of an isolated replay of Sam Snead's picture swing. Or Ben Hogan's.

Some doctors say the subconscious mind takes over while you are asleep and helps settle problems. Perhaps so. I know I did a lot of thinking and dreaming while lying flat on my back for weeks following that automobile accident. I guess I thought about Hogan more than anybody else because he was my idol. Paralyzed from the waist down, I would swing clubs in the bed and make believe it was Hogan hitting a fairway wood shot dead to the pin.

Golfers have more advantages in developing good images now than they used to. Almost every weekend there are filmed and live tournaments on television. The best in golf form is demonstrated free in the living room. It is no wonder that we are raising a breed of monsters who are devouring par and making life miserable for oldtimers on the professional golf tour.

Aside from developing confidence, the right mental image helps the golfer minimize the flaws in his technique.

2. BELIEVE IN YOURSELF

Confidence is the most important ingredient on the golf course, the baseball diamond, the football field and the track.

Without it, nerves become jagged and pressure builds up.

The best example I can think of to demonstrate the power of positive thinking is the four-minute mile. For years, it was an impossible barrier. Runners got close but the invisible enemy would slow them down in the last few strides. Finally, on May 6, 1954, Roger Bannister ran a mile in less than four minutes. Then came a rash of four-minute miles.

A golfer doesn't have to think he is doing something as noteworthy as running a four-minute mile every time he steps on the No. 1 tee but he does have to have confidence.

The most painful example I can recall of the power of negative thinking happened on the 16th hole of the Firestone Country Club in the 1964 World Series of Golf. I had a good drive and a fine second shot on the long par five hole. I had a 100-yard approach to the green across a pond. I said to myself, "if I don't hit this shot just right, it could fall into the water." Sure enough, the shot was short

5

and splashed my chances of staying in the running.

Too many golfers fret about hooking out of bounds into the road or slicing into a pond. The mere thought of disaster causes their muscles to tighten. Tension replaces confidence.

A golfer should get a mental picture of how he wants to play the ball and swing with ease and deliberation toward that goal.

It will do no good to picture the shot you intend to hit unless you have complete confidence that you can perform it. Remember, also, that if you happen to hit a bad shot or if you fail to hit the shot as you pictured it, don't let this discourage you or destroy your confidence for the next shot. Too many players let one bad shot ruin the rest of their round. You must be persistent and you must *believe* in yourself, shot after shot, day after day.

On every shot, before you swing and before you take your stance, visualize how the perfect shot should travel. Keep this image in mind. Approach the ball with determination to make your hands and arms perform the shot as you have pictured it. You will be amazed how often you will succeed.

The best example of the power of confidence on the golf course is Arnold Palmer. His mental approach to the game has offset any shortcomings in technique he might have. His confidence is contagious and has helped many a duffer improve his game. Pros, too, have benefitted from his think-the-ball-into-the-hole attitude.

3. HAVE A FREE MIND

Golf is a game of concentration. You can't have a lot of other things on your mind and play as well as you should. If you have an accident on your way to the course and your car is banged up, you might as well return home. You'll be worrying about whose fault it was or whether the guy has insurance when you should be thinking about whether you want to go for the center of the green or shoot for the pin. If your wife is about to have a baby, chances are you'll be on needles and pins. She will be feeling bad, awaiting the big

7

Have a free mind for tedious shots.

moment, and your game will suffer.

Looking back at the chart of my rounds on the tour, I can see where my scores dropped when I was concerned about my wife, Nancy. She was pregnant during the P.G.A. tournament, and she would walk around to get exercise. I would watch her out of the corner of my eye, especially when there were steep hills or slick places. And I was afraid she would be caught in one of those gallery stampedes and never have the baby.

Although golf is a business for the pro, it is a place for the amateur to forget the stock market and normal worries of the business whirl. It is a haven for exercise, relaxation and companionship.

President Eisenhower's devotion to the game as a means of strengthening himself after having a heart attack has given golf an excellent therapeutic image. As a rehabilitator, golf has prolonged lives, which is all the more reason for not mixing the problems of life with those of the course.

4. DON'T EXPECT TOO MUCH

Confidence is wonderful but some amateur golfers go to the other extreme. They expect too much of themselves.

Frequently, a golfer with a 15 handicap has miraculous luck and comes in with a score in the high 70's. He concludes that he has conquered the game and next time out expects to be in the 70's again. On shooting in the 90's, he becomes frustrated. His confidence is jolted and he is ready to sell his clubs.

The best policy for the average golfer is to accept sensational rounds with humility and try to remember what he did that was out of the ordinary. At the same time, he should cushion his mind with the realization that nothing goes down slower than a golf handicap.

Ninety shooters—and we have pointed out that there are more of them than any other kind—shouldn't be too unhappy if they average five strokes a hole. Some of us sometimes don't do as well. I had a 90 at Pebble Beach in the Bing Crosby tournament. The wind was impossible. The round wasn't as bad as the score makes it

8

His favorite putter.

When you hit bad shot, check backswing; don't throw club.

appear. My friends didn't want me to turn my card in but I told them a lot of people would like to read about the P.G.A. champion shooting a 90. Anyway, it doesn't deflate me. I hold the P.G.A. record of 64 with Jack Nicklaus and I believe I might beat it some day.

The golfer can play his best game if he gets all the breaks, and his worst is possible if he runs into high winds or bad luck.

5. CONTROL YOUR EMOTIONS

Golf lends itself to self criticism. In some extreme cases this criticism becomes temper tantrum and display of emotion unbecoming to a gentleman (or lady).

We are our own most severe critics, especially when it comes down to a situation like nudging a little white ball two feet into a hole. Golf is unlike other sports. The opponent never touches the ball. There is only one person to blame, unless the irate golfer wants to challenge the work of the greenskeeper or the man in the foursome ahead who didn't repair the damage his approach made on the green.

Controlling reaction to a bad shot is the most difficult task in golf, especially in the pro ranks where a putt can be worth as much as $18,000.

Pros and amateurs alike have a tendency to let one bad shot lead to another. I went into the 1964 P.G.A. tournament determined not to make this mistake. I had some really bad shots, but each time I tried to concentrate on the recovery shot. When I missed a putt I thought I should have made, I began immediately to work out a strategy for the hole ahead. I had many opportunities to blow up completely but I was able to control my emotions.

This control is what makes Arnold Palmer great on the tour. Most of the time he can shrug off a mistake. The Masters of 1961 was an exception. Palmer needed to par No. 18 at Augusta to win his second consecutive Masters. After a perfect drive down the middle, he hit a six iron into the trap. He thought he made a mistake by not using a seven iron. He was so mad at himself that he double-bogeyed the hole. Gary Player won the tournament.

Arnie doesn't do that very often.

All golfers should plan their strategy and they shouldn't let one bad shot disrupt it. A bad shot instills fear, and the better the golfer is able to erase the memory of it, the more his rounds will improve.

6. PLAY THE SHOT, NOT THE EVENT

Many golfers think too far ahead in amateur tournament golf. They play the event instead of the shot. Premature visions of grandeur often prove to be their undoing.

On the professional tour, in amateur tournaments, or in a weekend foursome, the most important shot is the next one. Don't worry about shining the trophy until you are in the clubhouse.

I read a story somewhere about one of the oldtime greats (I believe he was Walter Hagen), who would bait his opponents into making mistakes. He would say, "When you win this title, we'll

Don't worry about trophy until last putt is made.

Ben Hogan congratulates Bobby Nichols.

→

have to go on exhibition tour." The kid would become so preoccupied at the thought of an exhibition tour that he would forget to concentrate on the round and the oldtimer would destroy him.

Most golfers are too smart nowadays to be duped by this type of strategy. Some of them still make the mistake, though, of playing the event, not realizing that it takes 14 tee shots with woods, four tee shots with irons, four fairway wood shots, 14 approaches and 36 putts to put together the ordinary par round.

12

For the tournament player who doesn't concentrate properly on the immediate task, it will take a few more shots than par.

7. Choose Your Partner!

Fellowship can mean much to the amateur golfer. That's why the same foursomes play together for years.

Nothing can shake your poise quicker than an opponent who tosses irritating barbs for 18 holes. Like, "You'd better straighten up that hook on this hole or you'll be in trouble." Or, "Run it out, Jim," after you have hit a weak drive, the inference being that you have purposely bunted.

My advice is to postpone play if you can't find suitable companions. Back in my amateur days in Louisville, I knew a wonderful fellow who changed completely when he walked on the golf course. He was congenial but when he putted he was hard to get along with. He didn't want you to stand in front of him, behind him or to the side. Last I heard, he was still having trouble getting a foursome because he couldn't find anyone who would disappear when he was on the green.

13

Get feel of "the blade" before each round.

Nichols analyzes game in press room after round in 1964 P.G.A. tourney.

Unfortunately, you don't choose your playing partners in professional golf. Most pro golfers are discreet companions. They know everybody is out there to do a job and horseplay is at a minimum except during practice rounds.

I like to play with Ben Hogan better than anybody because he inspires me. I learn something every time I play with him, whether it be in practice or for real. Hogan plays only in the big tournaments.

I don't believe I would have won the P.G.A. had I not been paired with Hogan in the final round. Hogan's presence seemed to help me concentrate.

I always liked to play with Cary Middlecoff also, but now he is doing commentary for television.

14   On the amateur level, the point can't be made too strongly: don't

play with somebody if he bugs you. Golf life is too short to come into the clubhouse carrying frustrations that you didn't have when you teed off.

8. IMITATE THE RIGHT PEOPLE

Golfers come in all shapes, sizes and weights. They execute good, bad and indifferent shots with swings and stances that vary greatly in character. For that reason, it might be costly to try to imitate your partner or one of the opponents in your foursome unless it's to learn which way a putt breaks or something equally as elementary.

I have seen players who would hit a seven iron extra hard in order to tout their opponents into using a club less than the hole demanded, thus causing them to hit the trap protecting the green. Imitation might be the sincerest form of flattery in other places but on the golf course it can be treacherous.

On the tour, I don't like to watch my playing partners hit unless I have a similar shot.

In this connection, I might add that it's not wise to imitate everything you see the pros do on television. Most of them are experienced and can make a ball do strange things with a turn of the hand or twist of the body that you might not detect. Perhaps it is best to get a mental picture of the pros' rhythm and swing and use this as a basis for your own game.

9. ANALYZE YOUR GAME

If you are not playing as well as you think you should, get a map of the course and analyze your game. Make a diagram of each shot; you may be surprised at what it shows.

If you have wild shots early in the game, perhaps it is because you need more practice before starting play. If wildness comes late in the round, maybe you are getting too tired and have practiced too much. The diagram will reveal your inconsistencies and provide a basis for improvement.

It is possible for a player to be hitting his woods and irons well 15
and blow his game on the putting green without realizing it until

the putts have been added.

Wood shots and putts consume about 80 per cent of the average golfer's round, so I would recommend a close check on them in any analysis.

The Golf Writers Association of America has devised a golf box score that could be helpful to the amateur in doctoring his game. Here is the box for the final round of the 1964 P.G.A. Tournament at Columbus:

Player	PHP	R	BK	1P	2P	3P	B	Score
Nichols*	14	5	2	7	10	1	4	35–32—67
Nicklaus	17	6	0	5	13	0	7	32–32—64
Palmer	15	11	2	5	12	1	4	34–35—69
Rudolph	12	2	3	6	12	0	5	32–37—69
Venturi	13	4	2	6	11	1	6	36–33—69
Hogan	13	5	3	4	14	0	3	36–36—72
Lema	13	4	4	5	12	1	3	36–35—71

* Nichols eagled 526-yard 10th hole with driver, No. 3 wood and 35-foot putt.

Legend: PHP—Putting areas hit in par or less. R—Times in rough. BK—Times in bunkers. 1P—One-putt greens. 2P—Two-putt greens. 3P—Three-putt greens. B—Birdies.

This shows that Jack Nicklaus was getting the ball on the green with uncanny accuracy but couldn't get his putts to fall; that Palmer was hitting a substantial number of greens in regulations despite being in the rough 11 times and in the bunker twice; that Mason Rudolph was playing a fine short game around the green to offset only 12 greens hit in regulation.

When you have a bad round—and everyone has them—try this formula. Instead of brooding about it and becoming discouraged, think back over the round at the number of good shots you hit. The good shots will far outnumber the bad ones and convince you that a few bad shots kept you from having an excellent round.

16

It doesn't pay to gamble on doglegs. Solid line shows path of guy who was trying to get a better shot to the green. His ball trickled under a tree and he had to pitch into the fairway, losing a stroke. Broken line shows correct way to play a dogleg—straight down the fairway.

Study your bad shots with the constructive goal of eliminating the cause on the practice tee. Don't make the same mistake twice.

By diagramming your round, you may find that you were in the right rough more than the left rough off the tee. You can decide what happened. Or, perhaps, you were usually short on long putts or they were breaking to the right instead of the left.

A little trouble-shooting helps to streamline the next round.

10. Get Warm But Not Hot

Did you ever see basketball players come on the floor for the tipoff without shooting a few baskets and free throws? Or a football team go directly to the kickoff without loosening up with calisthenics and punting? Or a baseball team start right off without

17

Nichols points out 71.

Imitate the right people. A fan watches Nichols through periscope during P.G.A. tournament.

infield practice and warmups for the pitchers? It would be unthinkable.

So it should be with a round of golf. Any golfer from the pro to the 36 handicapper will find his game improved if he takes a little time to get the feel of the clubs.

Sometimes, the worse I practice the better I play. On the practice tee, I don't try so much for accuracy as I do for getting the proper rhythm and swing.

I would suggest that the average golfer start with the short irons and work up to the driver. Don't hit too many drives without resting between them. Driving takes a lot of energy. If you drive too much you will leave your game on the practice tee and be tired before the end of the round.

18

I taper off with a brief putting practice because if you don't get the feel of that important blade, your good driving and approaching will be of little avail.

During practice, accent the weakness you showed in your last round. If your handicap is 15 or above, I would guess that more emphasis on short approaches would shave five strokes off your round. Players in the high handicap area usually are short of the green in regulation. Accurate chipping can get them close enough to sink a putt for a par.

11. DON'T GAMBLE

Double bogey and triple bogey are ugly words on a golf course. They kill good rounds and frequently send the player into a tailspin with which he can't cope.

Often, bogeys stem from taking too big a chance or downright carelessness. In either case, they count the same.

Best advice to the amateur is to play it safe. If it comes to hitting a difficult shot over the trees and a chance at par or playing around them for less chance at par and a certain bogey, take the latter. Pros are frequently faced by such a decision and they play the percentages, that being the safer shot. If pros don't take a chance, then amateurs don't figure to gain much by gambling.

Shoot for the fat part of the green when the pin is close to trouble. It is better to hit the green and take two putts—the first of which just might go in—than to take a chance of having to come out of a trap or deep rough.

The dog-leg hole offers another temptation to gamble. By cutting across trees and flirting with an impossible lie, the long hitter takes a chance. His reward usually is nothing more than having an opportunity to use the wedge or nine iron on the next shot rather than the seven iron which he would have used had he followed the course architect's advice. The reward is not worth the gamble.

High handicap players especially should be wary of golf gambles. It is better to take a bogey rather than risk a double or triple bogey trying to go for par.

Nichols, a big eater, doesn't give food a chance to bother his game. He won't play after eating—at least for two hours.

12. GIVE YOUR MIND A CHANGE

How many golfers do you know who gulp down a big meal and dash out on the first tee for 18 holes of golf?

Too many, I suppose.

For the first nine holes, these golfers aren't giving their brain a chance to cope with playing decisions. Blood has rushed from the brain to the stomach to cope with the digesting of food, causing a feeling of sluggishness not conducive to the best golf.

It is no wonder that so many early holes are bogied.

If I am playing at noon, I usually don't eat anything after breakfast. If I eat just before teeing off, I get nauseated.

Most pros eat a heavy breakfast, then carry raisins, honey or a candy bar to sustain them. A combination of food and tension don't mix very well.

Since the P.G.A. tournament, I don't drink coffee during a tournament. I find that it helps my nerves and enables me to get a good night's sleep, which is important during four pressure-packed days.

Most of those on the professional tour don't drink, or drink in moderation. This would be good advice for the amateur, too. Some of the oldtimers might have won tournaments with hangovers but they couldn't do it today with these fresh, young and sober kids throwing well-honed bodies and well-trained minds into competition for big money.

20

Chapter Two

GRIP TRIGGERS ACCURATE SHOT

The grip is the most important facet of the swing. A faulty and uncomfortable grip can start a chain reaction that will send the ball in any direction. It is like launching a missile. If the triggering machinery is imperfect, the missile gets off to a wobbly start. It is likely to miss its mark by miles.

First of all, the grip must feel comfortable.

The grip is the golfer's focal point—the key to accurate golf. It is the only contact the body has with the club head and the ball. If all is not well with the grip, a message is sent from the "trigger" room to the brain and before the swing is completed, harassments have spread to the arms, knees and feet.

Naturally, if one is changing from the overlapping to the interlocking grip or is moving his hands to see more knuckles or fewer knuckles, the grip won't have that cozy feeling at first. This is understandable. Give the new grip a chance.

I check my grip before almost every drive. I do this to convince myself that all is well. If the knuckles and fingers are in their right

places, I have the image of a drive that will sail down the middle.

Control is another important item in the grip. It can't be checked by looking at the fingers and knuckles. It has to be done by feel. The grip has to hit a happy medium: it can't be too tight but it must be tight enough.

A grip that starts out right can go bad on the backswing when the fingers lose control. That's why firmness is necessary. It's like teaching your girl friend to ice skate. You wouldn't squeeze her hand until it hurt but you would grip it firmly enough to keep her on the right path.

A feeling that the hands are working together is another factor that generates confidence. If the brain is convinced that everything is working in unison, it will carry out a smooth backswing, down-swing and follow-through.

22

The interlocking grip.

I would recommend that the beginner spend a lot of time perfecting his grip. A faulty grip leads to hooks and slices that send the entire game into a tailspin, causing emotional upset that could have been avoided with a little practice in the living room. (I mean practice holding the club right, not swinging practice which would endanger the chandeliers.)

Of the Mental Dozen outlined in Chapter One, Nos. 1, 2, 3, 5 and 9 seem to be most applicable. You get the picture of the right grip, believe in the way you have applied it, don't let other irritating matters interfere and subject yourself to analysis when something goes wrong.

You hear the words "touch" and "feel" many times on the tour. They apply to the significant relationship between the hands and the clubs.

23

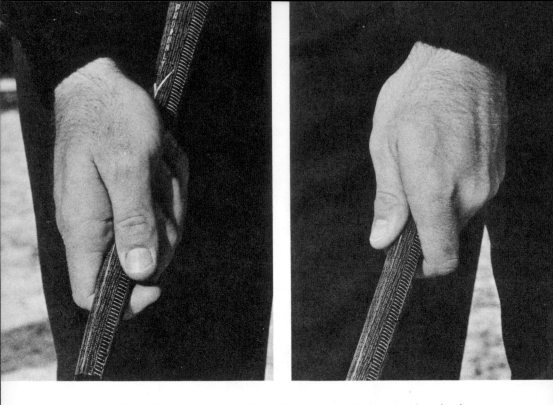

Touch means as much to the golfer as it does to the pianist.

Few pros have fingernails. They don't like to shake hands during the day of tournament play. Often, they use wet towels to make their hands feel fresh. These precautions preserve and even accentuate the sensitivity in hands which make contact with the clubs that guide the ball to birdie territory or bogeyland.

The friendly feeling generated between the hands and the clubs is the most important faculty in golf. If all is not well at this basic point, the rhythm of the swing can be disrupted and balance upset.

I suppose I am more sensitive to the touch and grip than most golfers because that was the only contact I had with the game for weeks after my accident. It doesn't seem like much but I got a lot of pleasure out of holding my clubs in bed. I could feel the life gradually coming back to my fingers.

Even so, I don't think it is wise for me or any other pro to say what is the right grip. That is a matter of individual preference.

Most professionals and amateurs today use the overlapping grip popularized by Harry Vardon. The little finger of the right hand overlaps the index finger of the left hand.

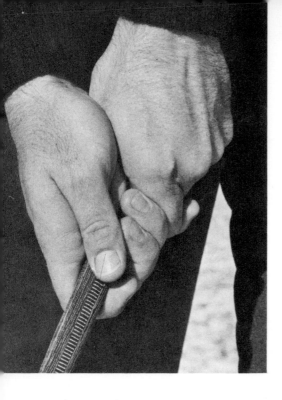

Right thumb presses against left side of club.

Left thumb is down the shaft.

And both are joined together in Vardon grip.

Jack Nicklaus gets good mileage out of the interlocking grip in which the index finger of the left hand and the little finger of the right hand are interlocked. Oldtimers such as Gene Sarazen and Lloyd Mangrum also used it effectively.

Another method is the baseball grip which has ten fingers on the club with no overlapping or interlocking. Art Wall and Bob Rosburg have made good use of the baseball grip.

Jack Nicklaus and Arnold Palmer are persuasive proof that grip is an individual affair. Nicklaus, who uses the interlocking grip, won $113,284 in 1964. Palmer, an exponent of the overlapping grip, had $113,203 in official money.

To emphasize the point that the type of grip depends on the size of the hands and the swing characteristics of the individual, let me mention that pros frequently change their grips. It is the first item checked when things go wrong. In fact, a standard joke among pro golfers is, "I like that grip better than the one you used last week."

George Bayer and Gene Littler are among those who changed their grip for the better. Bayer is the longest hitter in golf when he lets out.

25

I use the overlapping grip. I like to think of my left hand as a palm-and-finger contact and my right hand as a finger contact.

My left thumb is on top of the shaft but it hasn't always been that way. In my amateur days, it was to the right of the shaft and I had a horrible hook. I played a round with Ben Hogan at Fort Worth and he had me move the left thumb to the top of the shaft. It cost me about 15 yards on my drives but I hit straighter and the out of bounds on the left don't worry me as much as they used to.

Bayer had similar trouble.

I like to see two knuckles on my left hand as I look down at the grip. Some players prefer to see three knuckles and some one knuckle.

The "V" formed by the thumbs and forefingers should point over the right shoulder.

I feel pressure in all the fingers of my left hand during the swing but only in the two top fingers of my right hand. The right part of the thumb presses against the shaft.

The short left thumb fits cozily into the heel of the right hand to give the hands unity. The cozier the better.

One thing is important in the grip, whether you use the over-lapping or the interlocking. Don't grip the clubs too tightly. This will increase tension.

Grip firmly but if you feel strain on your arms you are over-doing it.

And one further word about alignment: the back of the left hand and the palm of the right hand must always face the target.

Chapter Three

GET SET
AND TAKE AIM

Good players usually position the clubhead behind the ball and square to the line of flight before placing the feet. This is a psychological gimmick that works. It instills confidence that the ball will leave the tee in the right direction.

Beginners—and some veterans, too—frequently are bothered by two things as they take stance:

Are my feet far enough apart—or too far?

Is the ball positioned correctly?

These dilemmas should be ironed out on the practice tee before play starts. The positioning of the ball and of the feet should become automatic.

There is that eternal mental turmoil as to whether it is better to widen the feet and have better balance or narrow the stance in favor of more pivot and longer distance. This is a matter that each golfer has to decide for himself; but the general rule is to get as much pivot into the swing as possible without endangering the balance. Somewhere, there is a happy medium.

One thing is very important in the address. It is the feeling that the weight is concentrated on the inside of the feet. This prevents swaying, a sad condition in which the body moves away from the ball and slides through the shot. The hips do not turn, as they should. Once this happens, power is lost.

I am about to make a suggestion that might scare the high handicap golfer at first, but in the long run it will be beneficial. I urge that he look at his stance in the mirror or see it on film. Many golfers learn that they are not bending slightly at the hips, keeping their back straight and flexing the knees.

Once the flaws of stance are corrected, the golfer has a vision of good address, which leads to an image of good swing, and consequently, a good hit.

In setting up the proper address, imagery (Mental Dozen No. 1), confidence (No. 2) and freedom from trivial worry (No. 3) are most important.

The stance is to good golf the same thing as the sight is to gun

The closed stance. The right foot is pulled back from line of flight.

The open stance. The club shows line of flight. The left foot is pulled back from line of flight.

The square stance. The feet are even with the line of flight.

accuracy. If you don't aim right, you won't hit the target.

The feet should be placed so that they are spread slightly outward and the inside of the heels are the same width as the shoulders.

I like the square stance in which a line drawn from the tips of the toes would point directly at the target. Frequently, I will hit from an open stance, in which the left foot is slightly back of the right foot, or a closed stance, in which the right foot is moved back of the line of flight. It depends on the situation.

The knees should be flexed inwardly and the body tilted slightly forward from the waist. Flexing of the knees keeps the weight on the inside of the feet. It should never get on the outside.

The left arm and driver make a straight line from the left shoulder to the ball. The right arm is slightly bent and is pointing toward the hip. This naturally makes the right shoulder lower than the left shoulder at the address.

The ball should be teed up on a line with the left heel. As the clubs shorten and the distance lessens, the ball is played closer—on

29

a diagonal line—to the right foot. The swing becomes more upright.

I turn my hips slightly when addressing the ball, the left hip away from the line of flight and the right hip toward the line of flight.

Most of the weight on the address should be on the left heel. The player should feel that the left heel is anchoring the swing.

The head should be behind the ball, as it will naturally be if the ball is teed on the left heel.

Here is one warning about the stance: don't position yourself too far from the ball. It will cause reaching and nothing could be worse.

I got into a bit of difficulty with my stance in 1961. Somehow, I was placing my hands too far behind the ball at address. This was causing me to sway. So, I began watching others on the tour. I noticed, observing from a position directly in front of them, that their hands were on the straight line from the left shoulder to the ball. My hands were behind the line and created an angle.

On moving the hands forward, I began hitting the ball with more solid impact.

Chapter Four

EASY SWING DOES IT

If a golfer has a sound grip and the proper stance, chances are he will have a good swing. It's not necessarily so, but if a solid foundation has not been established in the grip and stance, the swing is sure to be less than spectacular.

The grip is stationary. So is the stance. The swing embodies motion which brings timing and rhythm and the perplexities of moving parts into the picture.

This makes No. 1 of the Mental Dozen highly significant because if one doesn't have the picture of what a beautiful golf swing should be like, he will have a harder time putting together well-meant pieces.

The swings of Sam Snead, Gene Littler and Ben Hogan are good to imitate but if we could add three words of advice, these words would be, "Easy does it." You don't have to kill the ball to get good distance.

A feeling of relaxation is the key to good golf. If the average player would think of relaxing on his backswing, he would cut five strokes off his score.

Mental Dozen Nos. 2, 3, 5 and 9 figure prominently in the swing. Nothing boosts confidence like a smooth swing because it contributes to consistency. A smooth swing also reduces the number of bad shots which are so upsetting to the emotions.

If the interior and exterior disturbances are at a minimum, the golfer has stronger powers of concentration with which to adapt his game to the course he is playing.

ALL MUSCLES TAKE THEIR TURNS

I like to think of the golf swing as the effort of a well-coordinated relay team, with the muscles involved taking their turns to produce speed at the precise moment when it counts most.

If one unit fails, the effort is unsuccessful.

The guiding left arm must go back to get the power of the right arm as power flows between the heels and up through the legs and shoulders.

Head is center of "wheel." Left arm is kept straight.

Ever since I was a caddie, I have been trying to develop a smooth swing. I have run into many snags but it has helped me to watch such men as Snead, Littler and Hogan. Just about every pro on the tour has something praiseworthy about the way he hits the ball.

My education started by accident. I used to overswing. After I was hurt in that car wreck I cut down on my backswing. Then Henry Ransom, my golf coach at Texas A. & M., made me practice swinging my left to gain more left-side control.

In my second year on the tour, Don January noticed that I wasn't making a full turn because of improper hand position when addressing the ball.

Then Arnold Palmer taught me to concentrate on the front side of the ball, take the clubhead back lower and come through lower. This kept me from hitting the ball too high and getting cheated by the wind.

Left knee flexes toward right knee. Body uncoils, unleashes power.

I am indebted to a lot of instructors but it's that way on the professional circuit. Any golfer is glad to help a fellow pro in trouble provided he is asked to help.

The best way to start the swing is with a waggle that eases tension and touches off the fireworks. High handicap players would do well to make a few movements in the path of the backswing before actually starting the swing. This also insures a correct takeaway of the clubhead and gives the player the feel of the club.

It is necessary to think of the head as the center of a giant wheel. The head (or hub) must stay in place or the spokes will get out of line. My head moves slightly to the right on the backswing and back to the left on the downswing but there is no back and forth, up and down movement when I am hitting the ball well.

Everything should move together as a unit in the backswing. The clubhead should be kept close to the ground for 8 to 10 inches. The

Right knee turns toward target. The arms finish high.

left arm is straight and the right elbow as close to the right hip as possible.

The weight should be inside the left heel until the club starts rising on the backswing, at which time it begins shifting to the right heel.

I would like to repeat that the weight should never get on the outside of the feet.

I let my right knee bend toward the left knee in a sort of forward press to start the swing. As the clubhead goes back the weight shifts to the right foot with the left knee flexed inward toward the right knee.

The hips and shoulders turn simultaneously, the left shoulder making more than a 90-degree turn and stopping under the chin as the club becomes parallel (or almost parallel) with the ground at the top of the backswing.

The hips face the target. Follow-through is important.

In the meantime, the right arm is kept as close to the right side as possible.

The body is coiled to unleash its power.

A pause is beneficial at the top of the backswing, something which the high handicap players would do well to practice.

The first move on the downswing is to feel the left heel being anchored again to become the pivot of the swing.

The weight shifts to the left at the start of the downswing. The hips turn to the left and the right knee turns toward the target as the straight left arm pulls the club inside the line of impact and the right hand pours on the power as the moment of truth is reached.

But that is not all. The follow-through is important.

The right arm becomes straight after the impact. The arms finish high and the hips turn toward the target.

All professionals have different swings but there is one thing in common: rhythm and timing. This is what enables Chi-Chi Rodriguez to hit a ball almost as far as George Bayer.

If you sense that your rhythm is not good, I would suggest that your swing be adapted to a tune which you can hum until the kinks are ironed out.

This would especially be helpful to those who go back too fast on their backswing.

QUICK REVIEW

THE MENTAL DOZEN

1. Get the picture.
2. Believe in yourself.
3. Have a free mind.
4. Don't expect too much.
5. Control your emotions.
6. Play the shot, not the event.
7. Choose your partner!
8. Imitate the right people.
9. Analyze your game.
10. Get warm but not hot.
11. Don't gamble.
12. Give your body a chance.

THE GRIP

1. Left thumb is on top of shaft.
2. Right part of right thumb presses against shaft.
3. The "V" formed by thumbs and forefingers points over the right shoulder.
4. The short left thumb fits into heel of right hand.
5. Pressure is felt in fingers and palm of left hand and only fingers of right hand.

THE STANCE

1. The left arm is straight, making it an extension of the club.
2. The knees are flexed.
3. Weight is felt on the inside of the feet.
4. The toes form a line pointing to the target.
5. Head is kept down, still and always behind ball.
6. The ball is played off the left heel on drive and moved diagonally toward right foot as clubs and distance shortens.

THE SWING

1. Waggle to ease tension.
2. Keep clubhead close to ground on backswing.
3. Keep right elbow close to right hip.
4. Weight shifts from left foot to right foot.
5. Hips and shoulders turn simultaneously.
6. Left shoulder stops under chin.
7. Pause at top of backswing.
8. Anchor left heel to start downswing.
9. Left arm pulls the club down.
10. Right arm adds power.
11. Follow through with hands finishing high.
12. Hips face the target.

Chapter Five

WOODS ARE
SHOW WINDOWS OF GOLF

The woods and the putter have to be regarded as the show-windows of golf. Most fans at a big tournament surround the No. 1 tee to see who can hit the ball farthest. Later, they congregate around the 9th and 18th greens to see putting finishes.

This naturally puts more pressure on the professional but he doesn't mind the No. 1 tee bit as much as the high handicap player who shudders at the thought of more than three people watching him tee off.

I have seen players in the amateur ranks who were so terrified on the No. 1 tee that they would use a No. 3 iron to be sure not to embarrass themselves with a bunt down the third-base line.

This lack of confidence is understandable because nobody likes to look like a weakling but it can't be whipped by avoiding the issue. The high handicapper should practice driving so much that he can hit the ball solidly with his eyes shut. Once he gains confidence, the battle is won. He won't mind whether he is watched by his three playing partners or 3,000 fans.

These balls are placed to show the relative position of the 2, 3, and 4-wood shots.

Thus, difficulty with No. 2 of the Mental Dozen is solved.

Confidence is the most important factor in sports. It is especially a necessary ingredient in the playing of the fairway woods, where doubt frequently jolts confidence. Should it be a 4-wood, 3-wood or 2-iron?

The decision should be made on the basis of your ability to use the clubs in relationship to the difficulty of the lie. The average golfer is too optimistic. He should use a 4-wood instead of a 3-wood or a club with a notch more loft than he thinks he will need.

Once the decision is made, stick with it and go all-out. Pick out the spot where you want the ball to land and feel that you have just the weapon to put it there.

The 5-wood, a club that one never sees on the men's tour, has made many an amateur happy and confident. It has a larger hitting surface than the long iron and for that reason alone makes the player think he can get more muscle into the ball.

Some women pros swear by the 5-wood. It gets them out of a lot of trouble. Someday it will be a standard club for men as well as women.

While No. 2 of the Mental Dozen is most important, confidence is not everything. One must have the right mental image (No. 1), concentrate on the shot (No. 6) and be wary of No. 8 (imitation). Pros on television use the long iron when the amateur would be better off with the 4 or 5-wood.

LONG SHOTS ARE LIKE BASEBALL HOMERS

Not long ago, some of the top golfers on the pro tour were asked which shot they considered the most important—the tee shot, the shot to the green, the putt?

There were varied opinions.

Sam Snead and Arnold Palmer, two long hitters, agreed that the putt is most important.

I am torn between the tee shot and the putt. You need them both and without either your fortunes are not likely to be too high.

Fortunately, one of the faculties picks up for me when the other lets down.

The par shooter will take from 14 to 16 shots with wood clubs off the tee. In addition, he will use the fairway woods three or four times. The high handicapper makes much heavier use of the woods.

In any man's game, the woods are important. Their accuracy gives the player a chance for birdie putts. If the woods are not performing right, more pressure is placed on the putting and the whole game goes awry.

A player needs good driving and good putting just as the football team has to have fine passing to complement a strong running attack.

The driver should be the easiest club in the bag to hit because the ball is teed up. There is never a bad lie.

On the other hand, the margin of error is greater. One slight mistake on the tee can putt the ball in 25 yards of rough or lake or trap. This error can be more critical than a slight miscalculation on the green.

For spectator appeal—and golf is becoming more and more a spectator sport as well as a participant sport—the long drive is more dramatic than the putt. The crowd is awed by booming 300-yard tee shots just as it is the home run in baseball.

Because of the many component parts of the swing that have to be geared to perfection, more confidence is needed on the drive than any other shot. Tension arising from a lack of confidence can cause any one of them to go wrong. This is where the good-putt part of a man's game can help the drive. Nothing inspires more poise for the next tee than a difficult putt that drops in the cup.

Biggest mistake made by the high handicapper on the tee is going back too fast on the backswing. If he could tee the ball somehow so it could be hit with his backswing instead of his downswing, he would outdrive the pros.

A fast backswing disrupts the rhythm of the swing and is destined to get less distance because it can't possibly get the hands, shoulders, hips and feet working together as the good swing should.

Julius Boros, 1963 U.S. Open champion, has been a great boon to the fast backswinger. His swing looks so easy and lazy but gets the job done, proving that you don't have to hurry.

Here are some key points to remember in the use of woods:

1. The left heel must be well-anchored.

2. The left arm must be kept straight.

3. The head must stay behind the ball without bobbing up or down.

4. The hands must lead the club into the impact area.

5. The clubhead must follow-through, rather than stop, after impact has been made. The follow-through gives more distance.

Speaking of distance, one of the longest hitters on the professional tour is Jack Nicklaus. Jack holds the P.G.A. Driving Contest record—a mighty 341-yard wallop at Dallas in 1963.

Nicklaus gets his power from tremendous leg action. He also has a good 90-degree shoulder turn and strong hip movement.

Golfers who are not getting enough distance—and few are ever satisfied—should think about the elements of power: shoulders, hands, hips and legs.

42

Before going into fairway woods, I would like to suggest that

No. 3 wood	No. 2 wood	No. 1 wood
17 degrees	*13 degrees*	*10 degrees*
220 yards	*230 yards*	*240 yards*

beginning golfers use the two wood or three wood off the tee at first to gain confidence. Their big problem is getting the ball in the air. These clubs will do it and the loss of distance will not be too great.

Unfortunately, all woods are not hit off the tee with ideal conditions. Hilly courses produce uphill and downhill lies. Balance is the key to good wood shots and balance is hard to maintain when lies are uneven.

In trying to cope with hilly shots, keep one principle in mind: play the ball closer to the high foot.

Use a four-wood or five-wood on a downhill lie and play the ball inside your right foot. The two- or three-wood should be used on uphill lies and the ball should be played off the left foot.

Don't be too optimistic if you are a high handicap player. You may not be able to use a wood at all. It is best to keep the ball in play by getting it in the air. If the lie is not good, better go to an iron.

The ball has to be sitting up if a wood is to be used in the sandtrap. It is best to use a four-wood; otherwise the ball might catch a lip of the bunker before taking off.

43

With driver, ball is played off left heel.

On sidehill lies, move closer to the ball and flex your knees when it is lower than your feet. When the ball is higher than your feet, don't use all the shaft. You don't need all the club because the ball is closer to you.

The ball will slice when it is lower than your feet and hook when it is higher.

On all wood shots, think about what you are going to do—and not what you're trying not to do.

Chapter Six

LONG IRONS
ARE STROKE SAVERS

Many golfers ignore the long irons because they lack confidence in their ability to use them. This is unfortunate because the skills involved in practice with the long irons can help other phases of the golfer's game.

The long irons are the victims of a vicious circle. Beginners at first have trouble hitting the ball in the air with the woods. So they become proficient with the irons and leave the woods alone until they develop rhythm, tempo and know-how. Suddenly, they have little trouble getting the ball off the ground with the woods, then the long irons are neglected.

Worst part about it is they won't even practice with the long irons.

There are 14 clubs in the bag and every one of them comes in handy at the proper time. That's part of the game, to be able to determine which club is best for the occasion and to be able to get the most out of it.

The long irons are not really so difficult. As a matter of fact, they

45

With long irons, ball is played between left heel and center of stance. Position of ball shows where ball is played with these irons.

have been very helpful to me in a corrective way. When I feel that my tempo if off, I go to the practice tee and work with my 2-iron. I know that if I can hit with it, my rhythm has returned. The long irons require perfect balance and the swing must be smooth. Any attempt to rush the swing for more distance is fatal.

When thinking of the long irons, I believe it would be beneficial for the player to envision a sweeping motion like the one used with a fairway wood. Too many high handicap players feel that they 46 have to use a descending blow with the long irons. When this happens, the player inevitably hits too hard with the right hand, causing a deep short divot rather than a sweeping and consistent divot.

Perhaps this helps to give the picture of the long-iron swing. If any club requires a picture swing, it is the 2-iron or the 1-iron.

If you fear the long irons, I suggest an analysis of your game as outlined in Mental Dozen No. 9. You will see where clever use of them might save two or three strokes a round.

Practice can overcome fear.

LONG IRONS DEMAND PROPER FORM

In the long iron category are the 1, 2 and 3-irons.

The 1-iron doesn't come in the ordinary set of golf clubs. It has to be ordered special and perhaps that's the way it should be. It is the hardest club in the bag to control. I wouldn't recommend its use to the high handicapper or beginner. He should wait until he has developed smooth swing and rhythm.

No clubs are more demanding of the correct golf form than the long irons. The head must be kept down. The swing need not be as long as it is with the wood clubs but it must go off without a hitch. The hands must be ahead of the clubhead and the movement must be down and through the ball.

While it might not seem important, inasmuch as the ball has already been hit, the follow-through is vital. The hands must finish high.

Weight, as in the use of the woods, should be kept on the inside of the heels; the grip is the same as with the woods except a little more firm, and the swing never should be hurried.

Proper use of the long irons calls for the utmost in positive thinking. The player shouldn't think about what he might do wrong. Instead, he should think of where he wants the ball to go. It wouldn't hurt to think how gracefully a similar shot was played in the Masters, the P.G.A. or the Open.

The average player can hit a 1-iron from 200 to 210 yards, a 2-iron from 185 to 200 and a 3-iron from 175 to 185 yards. Distances vary widely but one thing is sure among golfers of all

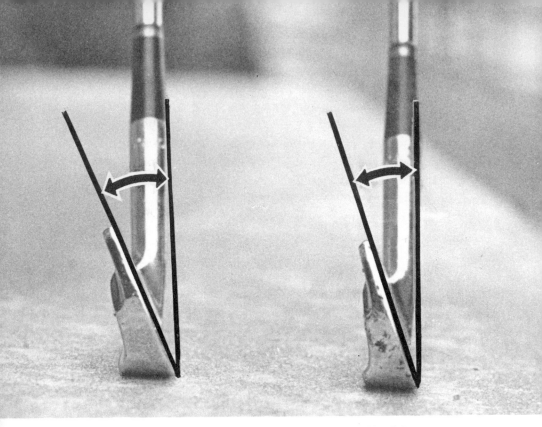

No. 3 iron
24 degrees
185 yards

No. 2 iron
20 degrees
200 yards

classes: it is not wise to try to hit harder for greater distance than the club's potential. This upsets the rhythm and leads to disaster.

Most players have a tendency to underclub themselves. They also think they have to scoop the ball up in order to send it on the right trajectory. They don't realize that the club's face is built to send the ball into the air if the manfacturer has done the right job.

On the tour, the 1-iron is a popular club when it is windy. Usually it is substituted for the 4-wood to make the 14-club limit. A well-hit 1-iron shot will cut its way low through the wind.

The 1-iron is also a "trouble" club. It is a handy gadget to keep the ball low under over-hanging limbs and yet get enough force to clear trouble.

The 2-iron is employed off the tee on short par four holes where accuracy is more important than distance. Such a hole is the No. 3 340-yard hole at the Columbus Country Club, scene of the 1964 P.G.A. tournament. The fairway tightens up at 275 yards out and comes uphill to a well-trapped green that slopes teeward.

After a good 2-iron shot that plays the percentages of avoiding trouble, it is an easy wedge from a level lie to the green.

I used my long irons only three times on the last day of the P.G.A. tournament but all three shots helped me win the title.

On No. 3, I used a 2-iron to the base of the hill, wedged to the green and sank an 18-foot putt for a birdie.

On No. 9, a 206-yard par 3, I hit a 3-iron shot on the green 14 feet from the pin and two putted.

On No. 17, a 219-yard par 3, I hit a 2-iron on the green 51 feet from the cup and sank the putt for a birdie.

The long irons and middle irons are birdie clubs, even though you do have to sink a putt to make it official. If you don't hit the green you don't have a chance for a putt.

Although the budding tournament player should practice until he has learned faultless technique in use of the long irons, I would suggest that the older player become proficient with the 5-wood and the 4-wood. They demand an easier swing and less power. Consequently, they are less disturbing to the rhythm.

Chapter Seven

MIDDLE IRONS
SET IDEAL TEMPO

Mental Dozen No. 1—get the picture—is important in every phase of golf but it is especially significant in middle iron play.

If a player isn't hitting his 4, 5 and 6-iron correctly, chances are there are flaws throughout his game. If he does hit the middle irons well, more than likely he has a good, all-round game.

The reason middle irons test your game is that they are used when conditions are ideal. Professionals and amateurs find the middle irons a perfect practice club with which to regain lost tempo and rhythm.

The middle irons also are good for beginners.

All these favorable features contribute to positive thinking and should instill the mental image of an arc dead to the pin.

MIDDLE IRONS BRIDGE GAP

The middle irons bridge that big gap between the long game and the short game. A solid bridge can lead to birdies.

For the novice, they are the best clubs with which to learn the basic fundamentals of golf. The reason many pros start their students with the 5-iron is because it has ideal loft. At the same time, the 5-iron demands balance, rhythm and tempo that is so vital in the manipulation of all clubs.

Accuracy, rather than power, is the main factor in using the 4, 5 and 6-irons. In fact, if you put too much pressure on the middle irons, you get into trouble. It is better to take more club and swing it in the right tempo than to try to hit a home run with the wrong club and lose your timing.

The stance is narrowed slightly when using the middle irons, with

No. 6 iron	*No. 5 iron*	*No. 4 iron*
36 degrees	*32 degrees*	*28 degrees*
145 yards	*155 yards*	*170 yards*

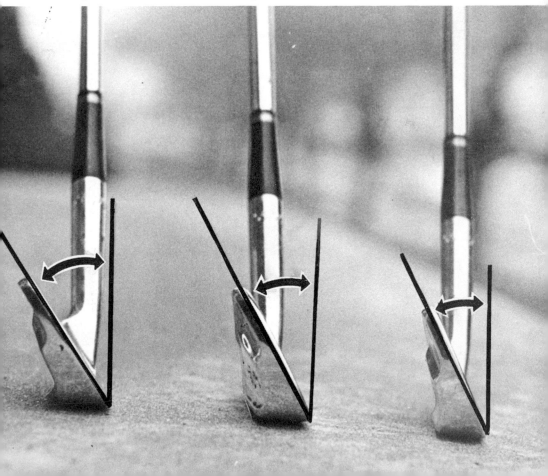

Ball is played in center of stance with 4, 5, and 6-irons.

the feet being closer than the width of the shoulders. The ball is played nearly to the center of the stance and closer to the feet to compensate for the shorter shafts. The knees are bent slightly.

Grip the club firmly and take the middle iron back slowly, making sure that it is low on the ground. When the hands reach waist high, the wrists begin to cock and the weight shifts to the right side.

The backswing isn't as pronounced as it is with the woods and long irons. The left arm barely passes the horizontal stage, and the right elbow digs into the right side.

52   After the turn is made, try to bring the club back in the same path it went up and don't hurry the downswing. Easy does it. That

is the secret of success with the middle irons.

The weight shifts and the club moves down and through the ball, taking turf after the impact is made.

Most important thing to remember is to finish with a high and full follow-through.

Be aware throughout the swing that the club will take care of the loft and that no movement is necessary except a smooth swing.

I feel close to the middle irons because they got me out of several tight spots in the P.G.A. tournament.

On the second hole of the last round, my drive hit the trees to the left but bounced back into the fairway. I hit a 4-iron shot to the green and holed out a 5-foot putt for a birdie, putting me ahead of Arnold Palmer again.

On the 15th hole, a 474-yard par 4, my drive caught the edge of the rough. It was a bad lie and there was a danger of losing control of the shot if I tried to hit to the pin. It was not a good spot to be in with Jack Nicklaus now breathing down my neck.

I decided to play a little hook on a 4-iron and make it run toward the pin. I had to hit the ball solidly.

Once I had planned my strategy I went all-out to execute the shot I had pictured. It was no place for negative thinking.

The ball rolled on to the green and stopped 15 feet from the pin. I made the putt for a birdie to restore my three-stroke lead.

A shot like this illustrates the versatility of the middle irons. They are the most maneuverable clubs in the bag.

In using them there are a few pointers to keep in mind. To hook the ball, move your left foot forward and swing from the inside out. For a fade (or a slice, to give it the more exaggerated term) open your stance by pulling your left foot back and swing from the outside in.

The middle irons are lifesavers when it comes to trouble. On a downhill lie, play the ball off the right heel and flex the right knee to give the correct balance. On an uphill lie, play the ball just behind the left heel and flex the left knee.

53

As I pointed out in a previous chapter, remember to play the ball closer to the high foot on uphill and downhill lies.

A sidehill lie is difficult, but once you master the necessary balance it becomes just another shot.

When the ball is lower than the feet, flex the knees more than usual, keep the weight on the heels and grip the end of the shaft.

When the ball is higher than the feet, move the hands down on the club, keep the weight more on the balls of the feet and play the ball toward the right foot, using a three-quarter swing.

If you are a high handicap golfer and a fair putter, I would advocate long practice sessions with the middle irons to improve your game. The closer the approach to the pin, the easier the putt.

Chapter Eight

SHORT IRONS
SET UP BIRDIES

As the ball gets closer to the hole, golf becomes less a game of brute force and more one of meticulous accuracy in which a well-placed 7-iron or 8-iron can set the stage for a birdie. Or an errant 9-iron can send the ball into a yawning trap with a protruding upper lip.

The closer to the hole the ball gets, the less are the chances of making up for a bad shot. This naturally puts a higher premium on psychological well-being.

But even the player who has the right mental image, is bubbling confidence, and whose mind is free of external worry is likely to tense up if he knows his next shot *has* to be a good one.

The most frequent mistake made with the short irons is underclubbing. High handicap players, particularly, overestimate their ability to reach the green with a certain club. For every one ball that goes over the green, there will be three or four which don't reach it.

When I'm under tournament pressure, I find it better to take a

55

club that will more than negotiate the distance and swing easier. This lessens the likelihood of a costly hook or slice. And it increases the chances of hitting the ball straight to the pin.

Getting the picture (Mental Dozen No. 1) is most important in accurate short iron play. If a player doesn't know how he is supposed to look while executing a 7, 8 or 9-iron shot, he is not likely to do it well.

The best way to get the right image is to practice. Most golfers don't devote enough time to their short irons. They like to boom out the long wood shots and hover over the putting greens but they ignore the clubs that could help save them more strokes.

High handicap players especially should concentrate on skillful use of the short irons. They're usually short of the green on long par 4's. A well-placed wedge shot or a neat chip could frequently save their pars.

ERRATIC SHORT SHOTS HARD TO MAKE AMENDS FOR

As stated previously, the closer the ball to the pin, the harder it is to make amends for a bad shot.

This obvious truth makes the pitching clubs—the 7, 8 and 9-irons and wedge—momentous in the route to par or birdie golf.

Professionals agree that the three most important clubs in golf are the driver, the wedge and the putter. High handicap players are not so keen on the wedge because it is a difficult club to use. But once you get the hang of it, the wedge becomes a true friend.

The short clubs are built for accuracy. The backswing is shortened, the feet are closer together and the stance is opened. The shorter the club—or the higher the number of the club—the closer the ball is played toward the right heel.

The grip in playing the shorter irons should be the same as the one used for driving. The grip shouldn't change for any club except the putter.

56   The swing is the same with the shorter irons but it is restricted to half or three-quarter because accuracy and not distance is the goal.

For 7, 8, and 9-irons, ball is played closer to right foot.

With the knees flexed and the weight on the left heel, the club should be taken back along the ground. It will start its arc sooner than with long irons and woods.

At the peak of the swing with the 7-iron, the straight left arm should be just beyond a position that is parallel to the ground.

The left hand should take the club down and through the ball with weight anchored in the left heel to insure that the head stays down and still.

Here is a warning: don't make an effort to scoop the ball over a trap or tree. Execute the swing properly and the loft of the club-head will send the ball into the air.

The short irons should be held firmly but not so firmly as to

57

*Ball is "pinched"
to give it backspin.*

produce tension. The right elbow should be held close to the right side.

If you are having trouble deciding whether to hit a full eight iron or to swing shorter with a seven, take the seven. Both of these clubs are clubs of precision, and undue effort to try to get more distance than they should provide, or any twisting movement aimed at helping the loft of the ball, will lead to trouble.

Many players get more control of the short irons by choking up on them, or slipping their hands down on the shaft.

THE WEDGE—"A SECRET WEAPON"

An oldtimer, asked his opinion about the record-breaking golf scores that are popping up nowadays, replied: "You have a not-so-secret weapon that we didn't have—the wedge."

Professionals spend more time with the wedge than any other club. It is no wonder that they have such a feel for it. Through practice, they learn how every twist and turn of the wrist and shoulders will affect the trajectory and spin of the ball.

Two types of shots appear to strike the fancy of the tournament gallerite more keenly than others. The long drive commands respect, naturally. But the crowd is also awed by the approach shot that hits the green with tremendous backspin.

It wouldn't be advisable for the beginner to try to put backspin

No. 9 iron	*No. 8 iron*	*No. 7 iron*
48 degrees	*44 degrees*	*40 degrees*
110 yards	*120 yards*	*135 yards*

on the ball until he has mastered the wedge. Though this is a valuable club it is also dangerous, and can make the ball do unusual things.

As to backspin, it is virtually impossible to put backspin on a ball from deep rough. High grass interferes with the clubhead and the spin of the ball after the impact has been made.

When the ball is in the fairway or even in the rough, if the rough isn't too bad, backspin is achieved by the upright swing of the wedge that comes down sharply into the ball. The club must hit the ball before it hits the ground. Otherwise, the motion is lost.

Sometimes, depending on the lie, the backspin can be improved by opening the clubface and bringing the swing from outside in.

The shot is difficult for the novice because there is small margin for error; but it is worth developing for the situation that requires a quick stop after a hazard is cleared.

Always keep in mind that the pitch shot with the wedge requires little body movement. It is strictly a wrist-and-arm affair with no turning of the wrists on the follow-through.

Chipping around the green is an art in itself. Proficiency can be realized only with practice, during which one gets the feel of the 5-iron or whatever his favorite chipping club.

The chip keeps closer to the ground, the pitch has more loft. The chip is performed most often with the 5 or 6-iron but the club used depends on the lie.

There is little body movement in the chip. It is all hands and arms. The same solid fundamentals of good golf prevail. The head must be kept still, the clubhead must hit the ball squarely and the weight should be kept on the left foot. The right hand does most of the work in chipping.

The big calculation in chipping is where to land the ball on the fly so that it will run up properly to the pin. No number of written words could give enlightenment on this fact of golf life. It can be learned only through experience.

60   I usually pick out a spot on the green or the apron where I want the ball to land and concentrate on hitting it.

If you want to avoid sand traps, then develop a sensitive short-iron game. If you can't avoid traps, the next chapter will give some hints on getting out of them.

Chapter Nine

WHEN TROUBLE HITS, JUST SETTLE DOWN

A good frame of mind is indispensable when you get into trouble on the golf course. Getting out of it is more mental than physical.

If you practice trouble shots in advance, a terrifying lie behind a tree, on a road or on a steep slope will merely become a challenge and you will rise to the occasion. Confidence will help put you back in "civilization."

Heavy rough probably is the most frequent trouble zone for the wayward golfer. It is fortunate that the average player never comes in contact with some of the roughs concocted for U.S. Open tournaments. At Brookline, an approach could stray five yards from the green and be in an impossible thicket.

Golfers on the tour never have agreed with the practice of growing jungles to ensnarl off-line shots in the Open. It simply isn't golf when the conditions of play are made abnormal. No weeds are grown in the outfield for the World Series of baseball. Floors aren't made slicker for the National Collegiate Athletic Association

Practice trouble shots.

basketball finals. The National Football League and the American Football League use snow plows and other heavy equipment to try to lessen hazardous footing on the gridiron.

I don't mean to imply that professional golfers want to be babied. They just want normal golf conditions.

Normal heavy rough calls for a little thinking. First things to consider are, is it deep enough to impede the club? Will it affect the flight of the ball?

If the answers are yes, then take these precautions:

1. Grip the club more firmly with both hands, especially the left hand. This will prevent the grass from twisting the club head.

63

For a buried lie, close clubhead and dig deeper.

2. Open the club face so that grass will offer less resistance.

3. Raise the club sharply on the backswing so that its descending flight will have less to resist before it meets the ball.

And, of course, keep your eye on the ball.

When debating on whether to use a wood or an iron to get out of deep rough, it's usually practical to choose the club that will be sure to extricate the ball from the bad lie. In most cases, this would be an iron.

HITTING OFF HARD GROUND

When hitting off a road or frozen ground, keep your weight on your left foot throughout the swing. This will prevent the clubhead from hitting the bround before it hits the ball, resulting in quite a

Follow-through with the clubhead.

jar to your hands.

Also, play the ball off your left toe when using a fairway wood off a hard surface.

HOW TO BEAT THE WIND

Professional golfers run into a lot of wind on the tour. If you have seen television of play from Pebble Beach, you know what I mean.

The luck of pairing and starting time can affect greatly the outcome of a tournament. Sometimes, players with an early starting time finish before a high wind develops. Or, the wind calms down about 1:30 or 2 P.M. when they are finishing their rounds, giving later starters better conditions and lower scores.

Take less sand on an uphill lie.

One-irons are popular when it is windy. They replace the 4-wood.

It is wise to use a club with less loft in the wind, cutting down on the backswing and insuring a lower trajectory. The ball should be played farther toward the right foot. This causes a lower flight.

And another thing: keep your head down to insure a solid impact. That can be said for every golf shot but it is especially true in the wind.

HITTING OVER TREES . . .

When a tree gets in your path to the pin, there's only one thing to do: go over it.

A wedge is used most frequently for this purpose.

The ball should be played off the left foot from an open stance.

This gives the shot quick loft because the ball is being hit at the bottom of the swing.

. . . AND AROUND TREES . . .

Frequently, when the ball is farther away from the tree but still stymied, it is better to play a hook or slice to go around the trouble rather than over it.

Apply the principles outlined before. To make the ball curve from right to left, or hook, close the stance by moving the left foot forward and hit from inside out.

If you want to circle the tree from the left, with a slice, simply open the stance by moving the left foot back and hit from outside in.

Before doing either, weigh your chances and take the lesser extreme.

. . . AND UNDER TREES

Sometimes it becomes necessary to go underneath the branches of a tree.

Best clubs for this purpose are the 1, 2, 3, or 4-irons. The ball should be positioned closer to the right foot than normal.

The club face should be closed to insure a low flight.

The hardest part of the tree trouble series is determining whether you should go over, around or under them. Once you make up your mind, don't change it. Go all-out to execute the shot to the best of your know-how. Confidence will help make it a good one.

HITTING OUT OF WATER

I wouldn't recommend trying to hit out of water. I would suggest that the average player drop out and take the one-stroke penalty.

There is a time and place for everything. Jimmy Demaret hit a perfect wedge shot out of the water on No. 15 at Augusta National in the 1947 Masters and got his birdie putt.

If the ball is covered by more than an inch of water, it is better to drop out.

If you must hit out of water, then keep the weight on the left foot and hit the pitching wedge slightly behind the ball. You won't get more than 20 or 30 yards but you might get out.

PLAYING SANDTRAPS

Somebody has said "eliminate fear and you have won the battle of golf." The most terrifying place on the golf course for most high handicappers is the bunker or sandtrap, whichever name you want to use.

I know amateurs who wouldn't dare try to blast out of a trap. They use a 9-iron and attempt to chip the ball out without touching the sand. This shot won't work half the time, especially when the ball is buried or when it is close to the edge of the trap and has to rise quickly to make the green.

I would advise any golfer, whether high or low handicapper, to practice blasting out of the trap.

First, being able to blast effectively gives much inner satisfaction. It's like finally turning on the big kid who is the neighborhood bully.

Second, confidence in blasting out of the bunker eliminates fear on the approach shot. How many times have you had such a horror of hitting the trap that you took preventive measures, which led to something far worse than a trap?

It is true, perhaps, that you have seen professionals on the tour fail in an attempt to blast out of a trap, leaving the ball in the sand. But this is a rarity. Actually, the sandtrap shot leaves a great margin of error. It is not nearly as hard as it looks. There is no prettier shot in golf than a well-executed blast from the trap.

And remember this one thought—swing slowly but firmly and don't try to scoop the ball out.

PRACTICE BLASTING BEFORE EACH ROUND

The best way to develop the positive approach to the sandtrap is to practice 15 or 20 minutes exploding out of traps before each round of golf.

Eye must be kept on spot behind ball during sandtrap shots; don't look up.

Be sure you practice correctly. Practicing the wrong methods is worse than no practice at all.

I got started badly in respect to traps. During the first two years on the tour I hit sand shots too hard. They didn't have any bite and frequently rolled across the green.

Then came Jay Hebert and the 1961 American Golf Classic.

I had practiced playing the ball toward the center of my stance and using a square clubface. Hebert told me to move the ball forward slightly and open up the club. This gave me more loft.

Then my putting picked up about the same time. I gained confidence and knew I could make a putt of 4 or 5 feet a good percentage of the time. That took pressure off my trap play. I started thinking in terms of getting the ball within 6 feet of the pin and the psychological effect was helpful. When I didn't think I had to blast

69

so close, my accuracy improved.

During the next big tournament, the 1962 U.S. Open, I landed in the sand 15 times and on 13 occasions holed out in two more shots. Sand doesn't bother me any more. I honestly think I'm going to hole out every shot from the bunker.

Playing the ball just inside my left heel, with my stance opened even wider than for the pitching wedge shot, I try to hit about an inch and a half behind the ball with the club moving from the outside in across the ball at impact. I aim a little to the left of the pin because the motion of the club causes the ball to move to the right when it hits the green.

The cut shot doesn't dig as deeply into the sand and gives more control.

First, however, settle your feet into the sand to get well-anchored before the shot. This gives you a chance to see what the sand is like.

Three important axioms of golf must be remembered in the bunker. Keep your head steady and follow through with the club-head. The knees should be flexed.

The swing is short but that will be automatically regulated by the open stance.

Sand is trouble enough but there are even more troublesome sand shots than the simple case of the ball sitting on top of perfect sand.

There are uphill lies, downhill lies, wet-sand lies and, frequently, the ball is buried.

For a downhill lie, the club must hit the sand further behind the ball and for an uphill lie, it must take less sand.

For a buried lie, close the club and dig in, taking more sand and overpowering the sand.

For wet sand, dig in about 2½ inches behind the ball and push the clubhead through.

Once you have mastered sand shots, you will get new satisfaction out of playing them. You'll save strokes, too.

Chapter Ten

PUTTING IS
A STATE OF MIND

J ust about every one of the Mental Dozen enters into putting.

You certainly must have the image of a putt delivered with a fine, smooth stroke. Above all, you need confidence in every putt. You can't think about your income taxes and get the job done; it is necessary to have a free mind—or, at least, a mind that is on the task of sinking that particular putt.

You have to control your emotions. Throwing clubs will only frustrate you and mess up the next hole, too.

The next shot must be considered the most important. If it is a short putt, you can't make up for it as you can a wayward drive on the fairway.

Choosing your partner has much to do with your putting effectiveness. I have seen pros who were so irritated by their playing partners that they would miss simple putts. Unfortunately, on the tour you can't pick your playing partners but club players can.

Other phases of the Mental Dozen, such as proper analysis of

Nichols strokes smoothly with $5 putter.

. . . the putt drops in at the last gasp . . .

. . . wonders if he gave it enough incentive . . .

. . . and Nichols gives victory whoop . . .

. . . the P.G.A. title (worth $100,000) is in the bag.

your putting game, the warmup on the practice green and bad
percentage shots on the putting green enter the putting picture.

It is on the greens that par is beaten or tied. Ben Hogan always
has said that "golf is one game and putting is another." He is so
right.

I have played well otherwise and putted badly and come up with
76's. On the other hand, during the third round of the P.G.A. in
1964, I played badly and putted well and shot a 69 that helped me
win the title.

There is a lot of luck to sensational putting rounds. When you
stand looking at a long, breaking putt, you must feel that you will
be lucky, too. Don't study the putt too long. The first line you
decide on probably is the best.

Just relax and keep your head still and concentrate. Once you
have squared yourself off, with the toes forming a line that points to
74   the cup, don't fret about direction any more. Concentrate on
distance. If you have noticed the pros, most of their putts are

missed because they are too far or not far enough. It is rare that they are off line.

My advice is to never play it short. The ball can't go in if it doesn't get there. On the other hand, don't be foolish and have a long one coming back.

Keep your head still until you hear the ball drop.

BIRDIE PUTT INSTILLS CONFIDENCE

The putting green of a major golf tournament is virtually a classroom in psychology. "Students" are convinced that mind prevails over matter on this particular strip of turf.

If a player sinks a long birdie putt in the early part of a round, it gives him confidence. When he thinks he can put the ball in the hole, his putting stroke becomes free of tension.

In the last round of the P.G.A. tournament, I hit birdie putts on the second and third holes. One was a 5-footer and the other 18 feet. I wound up making a 35-foot putt for an eagle on No. 10, an 18-footer for a birdie on No. 15, a 15-footer for a needed par on No. 16, and a 51-footer for a birdie on No. 17.

I will be the first to admit that I had some luck on those shots but it wasn't all luck. It took some skill and plenty of positive thinking.

In other words, successful putting is a state of mind provided the putter is reasonably versed in the mechanics.

Half of a golf round is played on the ground, which should make it easier than playing in the air, but it doesn't. A putter has to calculate distance, direction, slope, grain of the grass, dampness or dryness and, in some extreme cases, the wind.

Some contend that a good putting touch is born and not made. I don't agree with this theory. Anyone can learn to putt well.

I prefer a stiff-shafted blade putter without offsets or goosenecks. I like for my hands to be in a straight line to the clubhead.

I found a bargain second-handed putter in a pro shop at Anchorage, Kentucky, near Louisville. We made a hit with one another from the first. I used the putter in the P.G.A. and the Carling World Tournament. Now it seems like a member of my

Nichols'   putting grip.

family. I wouldn't sell it for a hundred times the $5 I paid for it.

You've heard of spot bowling. That's when the bowler finds a spot twelve or fifteen feet out on the lane over which he wants the ball to go. I find a dark piece of grass or any kind of mark that is between my ball and the cup. I try to roll the ball over the marker, figuring it is in direct alignment with the hole.

I also use the marker as a means of gauging putts that break downhill or uphill.

I line up the putt from behind the ball looking toward the cup, from behind the cup looking toward the ball and from both sides. This gives a line on any unseen breaks that might not be apparent from a distance.

Frequently you hear a television commentator say, and with great surprise, "that putt broke to the left instead of the right as I had expected."

You can't tell every time unless you look at them from all sides.

Stepping off my putts gives me a better sense of distance. Frequently, you can misjudge the distance as well as the break. And while walking off the distance of the putt you learn little things along the route that are helpful. There are hidden undulations and sharp breaks that you can't see unless you're right on top of them.

Putting stances on the tour vary as much as the types of putters used. I am not going to say that mine is the right one—my putter or my stance. But they have been kind to me.

I use a square stance, with the toes forming a direct line to the cup. My feet are close together but not so close as to throw me off balance.

Most golfers agree on the grip. The standard grip has the thumbs down the shaft with the back of the left hand and the palm of the right hand facing the cup. The left index finger overlaps the fingers of the right hand. This causes the hands to work as a unit, the left index finger serving the same purpose as the overlapping right little finger does in the Vardon grip.

My left hand guides the stroke and my right hand furnishes the power but both hands must work together. I use a shoulder-and-wrist movement and try to make sure that my putter moves well beyond the ball in a follow-through.

The head and body must be kept as still as possible. Only perfect balance can insure this. And the eyes must be kept directly over the ball, which is barely inside the left toe.

On an uphill putt, I play the ball off my left toe and keep my hands even with the ball and much of the weight on the right foot.

On a downhill putt, I play the ball in the center of my stance and make sure to keep my hands ahead of the ball. This change of weight and position of the ball and hands prevents scraping the putter head against the green.

When the grass is wet and the green is slow, I pop the ball with

77

Feet are close to-gether. Ball is played off left toe.

stronger arm action and when the green is fast, I stroke the ball gently.

The old theory about putting with or against the grain briefly is this: if, when you look at the hole, the grass is glossy, you are putting with the grain and the putt will travel farther than you think. If the grass isn't glossy, you are putting against the grain and if you're not careful, your putt will come up short.

In all cases, the ball must be hit squarely and the eye must not leave it until the impact has been made and the stroke is finished. I have seen many pros go into a putting slump and stay there until somebody told them they were peeking.

I would suggest more practice on short putts for the average golfer. I see them on the practice greens devoting much time to 20 and 25-footers. That's fine but the percentage putt is the 4 to 8-footer. If the average player can learn to make these with consistency, he will find his handicap dropping.

I probably am the last person in the world to say this because I have been called a slow putter. But I believe the average person takes too long with his putting. The more he surveys the situation, the more difficult the putt looks. This is bad for his state of mind.

Chapter Eleven

GOOD PRACTICE GROOVES THE SWING

Hitting two or three buckets of balls in rapid-fire order at a driving range, without method and with little concentration, is not especially conducive to making one a better golfer.

Such pointless preparation will give the feel of the clubs, but little more. Practice is for grooving the swing and ironing out the weak points.

The first practice should be held under the instruction of a qualified professional. Bad practice is far more harmful than no practice at all.

Practice sessions should rarely be longer than one hour—never so long as to be tiresome. If a person becomes fatigued, he drifts into mistakes that become a part of his swing.

It is best to start with the short irons and work up through the long ones to the woods. Although good form is the ultimate goal of practice, one should always have a target. With the woods and long irons, this target should be about 40 yards or less—the width of some narrow fairways.

*Don't hit too fast . . .
and too long.*

Although they are tempting, one should not hit from the high tees provided by the driving range. It is better to walk down the line and hit from grass, which simulates actual battle conditions.

All clubs should be used in a practice session. None should be used excessively, even if you are having trouble with it. It is best to take a few extra shots with a troublesome club, then go on to other clubs and come back to the troublemaker. The flaw may iron itself out with rhythm obtained from the other clubs.

Try to think of the shots you will need on the course you plan to play next.

80

Don't hit too fast and concentrate between shots just as you would on the golf course.

When warming up for a round, use only the regular shots in your repertoire. Don't experiment with new ones.

Most professionals work hard on the practice tee. Those who see them toiling either before a round or after one would dismiss the thought that the tour is a' life of Riley.

Most newcomers on the tour work harder than the veterans because they think practice can make them a quick success. But it doesn't work that way. The newcomers only tire themselves out.

Veterans learn to pace themselves. They try never to leave the best part of their game on the practice tee.

Practice on the putting green also can be overdone. Twenty or twenty-five minutes is enough. If you are stroking the ball well, even twenty minutes is too much because you might work yourself out of form.

High handicappers make a big mistake by not hitting a few balls on the practice tee and the practice green before playing a round.

The psychological impact of scoring well on the first three or four holes is significant. Yet, the high handicapper frequently rushes on the course and starts playing without even putting practice.

"I didn't settle down and play well until the back nine," is a common complaint.

And for good reason. The first nine was just a practice session.

Chapter Twelve

WINNING THE BIG ONE
WAS THRILL OF LIFETIME

Golfers get fired up like football teams that pull upsets and basketball quintets that shoot far over their heads. That is what happened to me in July, 1964, and it convinced me that the right frame of mind is the most desirable factor in sports.

I was hopping mad when Nancy and I left for Columbus, site of the Professional Golfers' Association Championships. An item in the *Louisville Times* had said some of the home folks were becoming impatient with me. They thought I should have already won one of the big tournaments, especially since I had finished in a tie for third in the U.S. Open at Oakmont in 1962.

As we rode along, I told Nancy I was going to win this one or not even make the cut. There would be no using of the 3-wood to play safe off the tee. I had decided to go all-out. I think Nancy had been getting a little impatient, too, for me to win one of the golf show-windows—the P.G.A., Open or Masters.

Anyway, I had worked up a keen desire for a big victory and the same newspaper article that gave me the desire helped give me confidence. It quoted Tony Lema as saying that I had the strokes to win a big tournament but lacked only the mental attitude.

The night before the P.G.A. tournament opened I started out right by observing one of the little things that sometimes make a big difference in the number of strokes consumed. I drank de-caffein-ated coffee with my dinner. I can't tell much difference between the real thing and the make-believe when I'm drinking it but I sleep better and my nerves are steadier when I leave off caffein.

I slept well and never felt so rested as I went to the practice tee the next morning I started with my short irons and worked up through the woods. My touch was good. I never felt readier for a tournament, even though I wasn't exactly sensational in that prac-tice round with Ben Hogan.

I was a little nervous when I teed off in the opening round but I soon settled down. The gallery was small.

I birdied three holes on the front nine. Nothing gives you more confidence than a few quick birdies. When you're under par and are not having to scramble to get back in the game, you swing easier.

My new second-handed putter was hot. When you make one long putt, it frequently leads to another . . . and another. Soon, you get to thinking you can't miss.

I birdied every other hole on the back nine and the crowd began to gather. The scoreboard back at the clubhouse always sends people out when a man is hot and a record is in sight.

I sank a 20-foot putt on No. 15, a 30-footer on No. 16 and a 15-footer on No. 18.

At the end of the steamy afternoon, I had eight birdies and two bogeys for a record 64 and led Jack Nicklaus and Mike Souchak by three strokes.

I was thrilled, and I didn't know which to thank most—de-caffeinated coffee, the $5 putter, the item in the newspaper, or, perhaps, St. Jude, who looks after hopeless causes.

During the first round, I had taken only 29 putts. That's border-ing on the miraculous, especially when you take into consideration

83

the length of some of those that dropped into the cup. I couldn't help wondering whether this was a fluke or something, and whether I would be able to keep pace the next day and prove to that huge gallery that I could stand the pressure.

The Columbus newpsapers played up the record P.G.A. round. It seemed like all of Columbus was there when I drove off to start the second round.

A professional golfer lives in a world of praiseworthy pars, beautiful birdies and electrifying eagles. They must offset the bitter bogeys and destructive double-bogeys.

I had decided to play for pars and let the birdies come where they would. I wasn't going to get reckless but, at the same time, I was going all-out to win.

I was comparatively relaxed despite the pressure as I got six straight pars. Evidently, I went to sleep. I 3-putted No. 7 and messed up No. 8. Then, I 3-putted No. 9.

You get a little jerky and start worrying a little when you 3-putt, especially if you have built up hopes as I had.

I woke up on the back nine and got two birdies to offset some of the trouble I had got myself into. By now, I was worried about Arnold Palmer. He was closing in on me. Palmer had a 68, thanks to an eagle on No. 10, and was only a stroke behind at the end of second round.

"This is my biggest chance to win that big one," I told my wife that night. "I must not blow it like I did the Open at Oakmont two years ago. I believe I have had my bad round. Thank goodness, it was only a 71. It could have been worse."

If I had known then the trouble in store for me during that hectic third round, even decaffeinated coffee would have kept me awake. It was weird and unbelievable. The score wasn't bad. I shot a 69 but hit only 11 greens in regulation and drove into the rough 13 times. How I came up with a 69 I'll never know.

I hit the trap on No. 1 but sank a 10-footer for my par. I hit into the trees and a trap on No. 2 and still wound up with a par. On No. 8, I had a bad drive and played down the wrong fairway. I wedged over trees to within 18 inches of the pin and sank the putt for a par.

I remember wondering if my balloon was about to burst and crowding out negative thoughts with the determination not to make two bad shots in succession. Hogan had once told me that the biggest lesson in golf was to learn not to let a bad shot disturb you. That piece of advice got a good workout as I scrambled around the 6,851-yard Columbus Country Club layout.

I made the turn one over par. I could have been four or five over and blown the tournament if I hadn't maintained the determination not to give up.

Chipping 65 feet to within two feet of the cup, I birdied No. 10. I made a 12-footer on No. 11 for another and felt that the tide of ill fortune had been turned. I 3-putted No. 14 and began to wonder again.

A miracle came on No. 15. I hit the rough with my drive, gained only 50 yards when my second shot caught a tree, ran a 6-iron onto the green and sank a 25-footer for a par.

A 6-iron approach that stopped 18 inches from the pin on No. 16 helped put me one under for the round.

My 2-iron shot on the par three 17th hole went into the woods 70 yards from the pin. The next shot had to be between trees and over a television cable.

"What happens if I hit the television cable?" I asked a tournament official.

"You will have to play it over," he said.

I had all to gain and nothing to lose by coming as close to the cable as I could. I hit a soft wedge shot. It barely missed the cable and bounced against the flagstick, stopping 18 inches away. I made the par. I also parred the 18th.

The nightmare was over. Palmer also had a 69 and was one stroke behind me going into the last round.

In the press room, I told newspapermen:

"Gentlemen, you won't believe what I'm about to tell you. Somebody up there was working for me today."

A sports writer asked if the fact that I could become the first to lead all the way and win the P.G.A. made the pressure any more unbearable. I told him I had my hands full worrying about winning and that records didn't matter.

Friends dropped by at dinner that night to wish me well. Escaping with a 69 after hitting so many bad shots on the third round was a tonic. I kept telling myself that I was due for a good final round. I went to sleep thinking how badly I wanted to win for Nancy and the new baby that was expected in three months.

Actually, two miracles happened to me on the next-to-last day. One of them was that I shot a troublesome 69. The other was Ben Hogan's 68. That score moved Hogan up in the standings, and according to the P.G.A. formula for making the pairings, I was scheduled to play with Hogan and Tom Nieporte.

It was a mental tonic for me to be playing with Mr. Hogan, the man I had idolized all my golfing life. It made me feel that the breaks were still going for me. Hogan had always been good for me—just talking to him or playing with him.

Even so, the pressure was tremendous. I knew that victory would mean $200,000 in purses, endorsements and contracts.

I was tied for the lead at the end of the third round of the Open in 1962 but then they played 36 holes on the final day and I didn't have overnight to think how much it meant to me.

I have never felt so much pressure in my life as when I teed off on the first hole of the last round. It probably showed, too, because I three-putted the first hole and Palmer was even with me.

On No. 2, I received my luckiest break of the tournament. My drive hooked into the woods. The ball struck a tree and bounded back into the fairway. It could just as easily have bounded out of bounds and cost me two strokes.

Inspired by this escape from the clutches of Palmer, I drilled a 4-iron 5 feet from the pin and made the putt for a birdie. An 18-foot putt on the third green put me ahead again but not for long. I bogeyed No. 7 and No. 8 and parred No. 9 and Palmer and Mason Rudolph were even with me.

"Was this the beginning of the end for me?" I wondered.

The gallery helped get me worked up for the occasion as I prepared to tee off on No. 10. I could hear them say: "Nichols is folding. . . . Here comes Arnie . . . . The Big Blue is blowing." (They thought I was from the University of Kentucky, which is called the Big Blue.)

I wanted to win, as much to show Mr. Hogan I could as for any other reason. After all, it was Hogan who had written me when I was about ready to give up back in Louisville after that automobile wreck.

I knew No. 10 had to be at least a birdie hole. Palmer had made an eagle there. The fans let me know it, too, perhaps thinking that it would cause me to fold.

I never have tried to hit a ball as hard as I did that drive on No. 10. It was a good one that traveled 300 yards as straight as an arrow.

My 3-wood approach stopped 35 feet from the pin on the 526-yard par five.

I read the green carefully. I was going for it but I wanted to get down in two. I stroked the ball and it rolled down the slope, made a big bend and plopped into the cup for an eagle.

That gave me the two-stroke cushion I needed and it might have taken some of the starch out of Palmer and Nicklaus.

I holed out an 18-footer on No. 15 for another birdie on a hole that had been kind to me.

On No. 17, my 2-iron tee shot came to rest 51 feet from the pin. A par would have won the tournament for me but you never know those things at the time. I knew that Palmer and Nicklaus, in the threesome ahead, were having good rounds.

I made the 51-footer for a birdie.

I still couldn't believe I had won after making the final putt on the 18th for a record 271. My margin was three strokes. It seemed like a dream and I was afraid I was going to wake up.

I didn't really feel the impact until Ben Hogan congratulated me, and I saw Nancy crying with joy.

Chapter Thirteen

PRO GOLF
IS FULL OF SURPRISES

One must be prepared for anything on the professional golf tour.

Like Arnold Palmer missing the ball in the Cleveland Open. Yes, the great Palmer whiffed and the stroke eventually cost him $8,000. It could happen to anybody, especially when the ball is in the rough like Palmer's, but it makes the duffer feel better to know that the most dynamic figure in recent years whiffs too.

And consider hole-in-one shots.

An average of 19 or 20 aces have been made on the tour every year in the last five years. At the St. Petersburg Open, two were made during the same round with Dick Howell and Joe Campbell scoring them on the same hole with the same numbered club within an hour of each other.

Even more odds-defying were two instances in the 1963 Palm Springs Classic. Exactly two years to the date after he won $50,000 for a hole-in-one on the 15th at Indian Wells, Don January used the same numbered club and made another ace on the same hole.

The last one was worth only a special $100 award as the "hard luck" player of the tournament.

In my first 15 years of amateur and professional golfing, I never made a hole-in-one shot.

Jack Fleck didn't get a cent for his feat of making eagle deuces on consecutive days on the 11th hole at Indian Wells.

They talk about weather a lot on the tour. It's either too hot or too cold or too wet or too dry. I would say I have had my share of breaks in this respect.

In the St. Petersburg Open one year, I shot a 69 in the opening round. Rain washed it out, giving me a chance to shoot a fourth round 64 that helped me win the title.

The rain came to my aid at Houston. I was three strokes behind Dick Sikes in a three-way playoff for the title. Jack Nicklaus already had been eliminated. Rain hit on the 16th hole and it might have bothered Sikes. Anyway, I birdied the hole and he scored a bogey. I caught him on the 17th hole and won on the sudden death 19th.

The grass was wet when we played the 19th. My drive faded into the right rough and the water held it up enough to keep the ball from rolling into worse trouble. I was fortunate enough to hit a 4-wood to the green and sink a 10-foot putt for an eagle and the championship.

One year the sponsors of the Phoenix Open took out rain insurance, which didn't seem necessary there. The policy expired at 2 P.M. during Sunday's final round. Fifteen minutes later, a violent wind and hail storm swept the course and forced cancellation of the round.

The weather played even stranger tricks during the 1962 Sahara Invitational at Las Vegas. The professionals in the first half of the field who played their first rounds at the Las Vegas Municipal course had swung away all day in the sunshine. Hours later, they learned to their surprise that a thunderstorm had visited Paradise Valley Country Club on the other side of the city, drenched the rest of the contestants and washed out the entire round. One of the poorer scores rained out was Tony Lema's 75. The next day he shot 69 and went on to win the tournament.

One of the oddest things happened to Raymond Floyd. During the first nine stops of the 1963 winter tour he didn't earn a penny. Then, he won the St. Petersburg Open to become the youngest golfer to land a title on the tour in more than 34 years. He was 20.

Al Geiberger is still shaking his head over this instance in an Insurance City Open. Teeing off last in his threesome, Geiberger eagled the 482-yard second hole at Wethersfield Country Club but still had to tee off third on the next hole. His playing partners, Julius Boros and Chi Chi Rodriguez, also eagled the second.

Pete Cooper put a shot into a purse of a woman spectator in a gallery moving ahead of him in the Western Open in Pittsburgh.

Ken Venturi bounced a tee shot into the back pocket of another player in front of him at Oklahoma City.

A dog picked up Paul Harney's shot onto the 13th green one year in the Masters.

And I will never forget what happened to tour freshman Binky Mitchella in the final round of the 1964 Phoenix Open. On the third hole, the Texan pounded three tee shots out of bounds and eventually sank a 30-foot putt for a 10. Then, four holes later, he watched his 3-wood second shot carry the remaining distance of the 529 yards from tee to flagstick and drop into the cup for a rare double-eagle!

GOLF IS FREE OF FIXES

The professional golf tour never has been involved in a fix scandal like that which rocked college basketball in the early 1950's. It would be impossible to fix a golf tournament because any one of 100 or so players is capable of winning.

I was approached, however, by a would-be fixer in an amateur tournament—the River Road Invitational—in the late 1950's Why any one would want to fix an amateur I don't know. Perhaps, the man had made a wager that I wouldn't win. He was taking a big

90

chance because a person convicted of attempting to bribe an athlete in Kentucky is guilty of a felony under a law enacted by the State Legislature after the basketball scandals. The punishment is not less than a year nor more than 10 years and a $10,000 fine. Most states have adopted similar penalties.

On the No. 6 par-four hole, the fellow whom I did not recognize offered me $75 to hit the ball out of bounds and take six strokes.

"I might take a six," I told him, "but I'll be going for a birdie or par."

I parred the hole and didn't see the man anymore.

Jouett Brown, the eventual winner of the tournament, was offered a bribe not to win. When he was in second place, on the final day, Brown was asked by a different man, "How much is it worth to finish second?"

I was playing with Brown at the time. He thought the guy was kidding until he pulled out a roll of bills and offered Brown $100.

Brown told him to go to hell and walked to the next tee.

More than likely the men had side bets against us.

We reported the incidents and the police made an investigation. I don't know what happened to the men. Joe Dey, executive secretary of the United States Golf Association, asked for a full report. It must have been the first attempt in history to try to bribe an amateur golfer—at least, Mr. Dey said it was so unusual that the U.S.G.A. had no rules for such an occurrence.

Nothing similar has ever happened during my golf career.

I remember those voices on the ninth hole of the last round of the P.G.A. tournament. I mean the ones which said, "Nichols is choking." Those men probably were betting against me, but they only made me more determined than ever to win.

I don't know of any professional tournaments on which odds are quoted except the one at Las Vegas. Bookmakers there will give odds on anything.

Stakes are so high that professional golfers don't need to bet among themselves. Too much money is riding on every putt.   91

Everybody knows there is penny-ante betting on the club level, where the handicap brings two players of different abilities together in a life-and-death struggle. Golf has this advantage over tennis and other games. The golf handicap is an accurate leveler.

It would be safe to surmise that three out of.four foursomes teeing off at a country club have wagers. Most of the time it is harmless dollar-dollar-dollar Nassau. This means that the twosomes bet $1 on the winner of the first nine, $1 on the winner of the second and $1 on the 18 holes. The maximum loss is $3.

Bingle-bangle-bungle is another popular game among the country club set. It is also a good game for players of unequal abilities. The player getting on the green first gets a fixed amount, the player whose ball is nearest the pin after all balls are on the green collects, and the player sinking the first putt wins, too. These forms of betting are usually harmless. Anyway, the winners buy the drinks at the 19th hole.

Big tournaments are on television, so it is natural that office jackpots on golf have sprung into popularity.

For me, the most interesting type of jackpot is the kind Ben Hogan plays during a practice round. Mr. Hogan likes to play it this way: the golfer in the foursome who misses a fairway puts a dollar in the pot, the one missing a green contributes a dollar. Each person keeps his own score and at the end of the round the player who has had to contribute the fewest dollars gets the entire pot.

Last time I had a practice round with Hogan I had contributed eight dollars on the first four holes; and you can't get any worse than that.

Hogan is usually quiet when he plays, even in practice. The only thing he ever says to me is:

"You're away."

And he's usually right.

FAMILY SUFFERS ON PRO TOUR

A woman's place is in the home and a pro golfer's home is where he hangs his hat. This works out fine when there are no children. Newlyweds find it romantic going from one city to another, meeting new couples and dining at the country clubs. It's a plush life.

The first child changes all that. A woman gets tired of being a baby-sitter. And it's murder to travel long distances in an automobile with a child or children.

A pro golfer on tour is unhappy without his wife. Hotel and motel rooms can be lonely. Yet, when the wife and children are along, the harassments frequently upset his game. He can't win either way.

So, a golfer on the tour winds up spending half of his time away from home.

There seems to be no real solution to the problem. It is a professional drawback, like being a traveling salesman or an airline pilot.

Most wives get baby-sitters or relatives and follow their husbands in the big tournaments like the Masters, U.S. Open and P.G.A. In the other tournaments, they stay home and call the newspaper to find out what their husbands shot that day. And golfers are the telephone company's biggest customers. They call every night to find out whether junior still has a fever or if the mother-in-law is still with them.

I have been very fortunate. Nancy was with me during most tournaments the first five years. Now that we have two sons, Robert Craig and Richard Dean, she attends only the big ones.

Nancy works harder than I do during a big golf tournament. She stays behind the ring of spectators around the green and doesn't watch me putt. Instead, she listens to the crowd. She has learned to detect from the oh's and ah's and applause whether I make a crucial shot.

After the P.G.A. of 1964, she remarked: "I don't think I've ever gone through one like this. He was in trouble all the way and that worried me."

That's the only time I have ever been really worried about her. She was six months pregnant then, and I was afraid the excitement might be too much for her. I could see her crying during those last four holes as I got closer and closer to my first big tournament win. I confess, it made me try a lot harder.

Wives following their husbands on the tour have a difficult time in another way. Nobody knows them standing in the gallery and they hear remarks about their husbands that make their blood boil. Some of them have become accustomed to it but others still bristle when a galleryite says, "That guy is a bum," and points to their husbands.

Most wives learn not to talk about golf when their husbands come home. They wouldn't dare say:

"Well, what happened today? How do you think we can pay for this furniture with a lousy 74?"

That would bring on disaster. Many of them use the tactful approach, like:

"Don't worry, honey. It doesn't matter. You can make up for it tomorrow—or next week."

By then, the golfer has had time to brood about his plight and shouts:

"What do you mean, it doesn't matter. You know that if I don't start winning soon I'm going to have to get a club pro job."

The wife can't win, either.

Most wives of golfers don't play golf but some of them probably would like to. I remember hearing Julius Boros' wife say she asked Julius: "How about playing golf with me today, honey, you haven't anything else to do." And Julius replied: "What! Play again today? You played only last month."

Best player among the golfers' wives is Vivienne Player, wife of the talented Gary. Mrs. Player had a two handicap before she started raising a family.

Gary credits Vivienne with helping him finish second in the 1958 U.S. Open. Vivienne noticed, after Gary had putted badly in the first round, that he was lifting his putter on the backswing. He corrected the flaw and closed fast.

GOLFERS HAVE VARIED HOBBIES

For relaxation, a large number of the nation's pro golfers content

Nancy Nichols, right, and sister Shirley Berg watch during P.G.A. tournament.

themselves with such light activities as reading, television, motion pictures and occasional change-of-pace activities like bowling and bridge and poker.

Other playing members go in strong for hobbies.

Arnold Palmer likes flying and has mastered it just as he did the game of golf. He has turned his hobby into a means of getting from one tournament to another.

Charley Sifford finds enjoyment during the off-course hours at a tournament in the fine music he records on tapes and plays back while relaxing after a hard day's work at the club.

Bo Wininger is an avid hunter. He has already experienced the thrill of bringing down a grizzly bear.

Julius Boros, George Bayer, Bob McCallister and Sam Snead enjoy leisure hours with fishing rods in their hands. Snead and baseball's Ted Williams made up one of the nation's most celebrated fishing teams in years past.

Bill Casper's penchant for fishing gained national attention when he won the U.S. Open. There were stories which told of how he would rather spend his time off the golf course and the tournament trail trying to hook a bass than hook a bag of golf balls off a practice tee.

Gary Player is a hi-fi fan. Lionel Hebert likes to make his own music. A talented trumpet player who majored in music at Louisiana State University and once had his own band, Herbert relishes the occasional opportunities that come to him on the tour.

Ken Venturi plays the drums. Venturi also is the fastest gun on the tour. He has accumulated many firearms. Johnny Pott and Bob Goetz, like Palmer, are addicts of the wild blue yonder.

A great many professionals, however, are so busy playing golf for a living that they have little time for extracurriculars. With them, golf is a demanding business.

Getting a lesson from P.G.A. golf champion Bobby Nichols is his 2-year-old son, Craig, at Miami. Bobby is in Doral International.

GOLF GROWS IN SCHOOLS, INDUSTRY

For a growing youngster seeking a hobby—or a prospective vocation—I can't recommend golf too strongly. Golf is being taught in physical education programs of junior and senior high schools. Colleges have gone for the sport in a big way.

Golf has become an integral part of every community. Major industry is building more facilities for its employees and encouraging competition among them as a means of preventing the all-work-and-no-play-dull-boy complex.

The outlook is for a 25 or 30-hour work week by 1980. By then, the number of golf courses is expected to be tripled.

These factors make golf as a career appetizing, especially if junior likes golf.

However, I don't think he should be pushed into golf until he wants to play. If he is exposed to the game, he will know whether he will like it or not. Too much encouragement might give him an attitude that it is something like spinach.

Things usually work out for the best. If I hadn't had that automobile wreck in 1952, I might have taken up football or basketball seriously. If I had, I don't believe I would have been able to do as well with golf, because it is such a demanding sport.

Golf has many advantages as a sport for youngsters.

First, he doesn't have to be seven feet tall. If he were, it would be a handicap. Timing and rhythm are more important than strength.

Golf instills self reliance in a youngster because he can't blame his teammates when he makes a mistake. He is on the tee or green solely in command of the club and only he is responsible.

Another advantage of golf for a kid is the company he meets. The conduct around a golf course is far better than average and the sportsmanship is superb.

The exercise is wonderful. Medics have established the fact that few exercises beat just plain walking.

98 Golf can be very rewarding for a youngster who becomes proficient at it. Club pros average $15,000 or $20,000 a year.

On top of that, the good golfer makes good business contacts that would not be possible otherwise.

I hope my boys take up the sport as soon as they are able to hold a club. But I'm not going to push them.

Bob Rosburg played baseball at Stanford and Mike Souchak was a football star at Duke. They concur in the belief that golf demands more mental discipline than any other sport.

Said Souchak:

"There's no comparison. In team sports like football, the rest of the players can carry along a few who might not have the proper attitude. And things happen so fast on a football field that you don't have time to stop and think. Your reactions are instinctive. On a golf course, though, you have to give a lot of thought to every move. If you can't think a winning game you're not going to win, no matter how perfect your swing might be."

Chapter Fourteen

ALL-AMERICAN COURSE
WITH PLAYERS TO MATCH

Wonder what an All-American golf team would do against the 18 best holes in the country, each player taking only the shots at which he specializes?

For instance, I can't imagine a better combination for the 620-yard monster at Firestone than Jack Nicklaus hitting off the tee, Tony Lema creaming a fairway wood just short of the water, Billy Casper dropping a short iron shot close to the pin and Bob Charles sinking the putt for a birdie.

Not long ago, *Sports Illustrated* picked "the best 18 golf holes in America."

The magazine picked its holes on the basis of their numbers. For instance, the best No. 1 hole was chosen over other No. 1 holes. The fallacy of this method is that the second best hole in America could be left out if it were a No. 1 hole and hardly as good as the No. 1 hole chosen.

Sports Illustrated also did not include what I regard as one of the best golf courses in America—the Firestone Country Club at

Akron. I believe Firestone and Augusta National, the site of the Masters, are the greatest tests of golf in America.

My All-American layout includes two holes from Augusta National and one from Firestone. Here it is:

FIRST NINE				
Hole No.	*Par*	*Length*	*Course*	*Location*
5	4	459	Colonial .... Fort Worth, Texas
5	4	438	Pinehurst .... Pinehurst, N.C.
9	5	538	Champions .... Houston, Texas
3	3	220	Olympic Club .... San Francisco
1	4	360	Merion .... Ardmore, Penn.
4	3	183	Baltusrol .... Sprinfield, N.J.
15	5	520	Augusta National .... Augusta, Ga.
12	4	470	Country Club .... Brookline, Mass.
6	4	388	Seminole .... Palm Beach, Fla.
SECOND NINE				
1	4	442	Winged Foot .... Mamaroneck, N.Y.
16	3	222	Cypress Point .... Pebble Beach, Cal.
12	3	155	Augusta National .... Augusta, Ga.
13	5	595	The Dunes .... Myrtle Beach, S.C.
14	4	460	Cherry Hills .... Denver, Colo.
15	4	458	Oakmont Country Club .. Oakmont, Penn.
16	5	620	Firestone .... Akron, O.
16	4	405	Oakland Hills .... Birmingham, Mich.
18	4	437	Doral Country Club .... Miami, Fla.

I'm not sure how well I could play this course but it would be a pleasure to try.

The two most fascinating holes on my All-American course are the longest and shortest.

The 620-yard monster at Akron has been good to me most of the time, but it ruined my hopes of winning the World Series of Golf in 1964.

It is a dogleg left, with a sandtrap on the right side of the fairway and trees on the left. There is another trap about where the second

101

shot would land.

The small, egg-shaped green is guarded by a pond.

The only sane way to play it is to hit a well-placed drive, a perfect 4-wood short of the pond and a chip onto the green. I tried to play it too close in the World Series of Golf and instead of getting a birdie, I wound up in the water with a double bogey.

A triple bogey there in 1960 cost Arnold Palmer a chance at the P.G.A. title.

Anything from a 4-iron to a 9-iron is used on Augusta's tricky No. 12, where wind currents make the ball do peculiar things. A creek runs in front of the green. There are sandtraps and rough grass in the back. Most golfers feel fortunate to escape with a par on this hole.

The 15th at Augusta is another water hole. A deep pond guards the front of the steeply elevated green and there is water back of the green, too. So, it's a gamble whether to go for the green on the second shot of the 520-yard hole or not.

Gene Sarazen got his famous double eagle on the 15th in 1935 and went on to tie Craig Wood and beat him in a playoff for the Masters title. It has been a turning point in the Masters.

The Doral Country Club has a fine finishing hole. It is a 437-yard par 4 with a long, snaky fairway and a lake on the left. The lake juts strongly into the fairway near the green and borders it on the left and in front and back. To the right of the green is a trap. Water, wind and sand are trademarks at Doral.

The 13th hole at the Dunes is one of the most awesome looking things in America. It is a 595-yard dogleg played entirely around water. A long second shot has to be played across the water to set up a third shot to the green. Every tough hole, it seems, is named Waterloo. This one fits the description.

Speaking of water, there's that 222-yard par 3 at Cypress. It requires a carry over the Pacific Ocean. This wouldn't be too bad if the wind didn't carry the ball to strange places. The late Porky Oliver once had a 16 here—yes, a 16, on the 16th hole.

The 15th at Oakmont is a 458-yard par 4 that's even tougher

than it looks. The right approach areas slant deeply toward a tremendous trap that starts 30 yards out. Wind conditions play havoc with the second shot. This chaotic condition follows a blind tee shot up a hill.

I was tied with Arnold Palmer and Jack Nicklaus for the U.S. Open title in 1962, with four holes to go. Unfortunately, this was one of the holes.

The No. 1 hole at Merion is a similar hole, shorter and a sharper dogleg but equally as demanding on the second shot. The 360-yard, well-trapped hole is a good one to start on. It is not as hard as most of the holes in this All-American layout if you have a good second shot.

The No. 6 par 4 388-yard affair at Seminole has more desert than fairway. It is a dogleg left that also requires a spectacular second shot.

No. 5 at Colonial is one of my favorites. The fairways of this 459-yard par 4 strip are lined with trees. Trinity River is an additional hazard on the right. If it weren't a dogleg right, it would look like a bowling lane.

When you play No. 9 at Champions Golf Club in Houston, you wonder if you'll ever find the green. It is nestled between trees and water, way back on the left side, 538 yards from the tee. A ditch and giant oak tree complicate matters. They're in the fairway and make almost every shot a gamble.

Cherry Hills at Denver has a fascinating hole in No. 14, a 460-yard par 4 that doglegs left to an undulating green protected by trees and a creek.

Oakland Hills in Birmingham, Michigan, is one of my favorite courses. That's where I won the $35,000 Carling Open. One of its finest holes is No. 16, a 405-yard lake hole. The second shot must carry the water and find a green surrounded by bunkers.

The 12th at Brookline, which members of the Country Club play as a par 5, was a rugged par 4 of 470 uphill yards for the U.S. Open tournament of 1963.

Baltusrol has an intriguing little par 3 which is like No. 16 at

103

Augusta. It is 183 yards over a lake to a two-level green.

Olympic Club's 220-yard downhill par 3 is entirely different in character from either of these but it is equally as colorful. It is lined with pine, cypress and fir trees. After this jungle has been conquered, a desert surrounds the fast green.

No. 5 at Pinehurst and No. 1 at Wingfoot are truly great holes.

It's hard to describe what makes a great golf hole. For some it is one thing and others another. I like a challenge and there are 18 challenges here.

MY ALL AMERICAN GOLF TEAM

There are, perhaps, 100 or so combinations that could be named to an All-American Golf Team, and one would be as effective as another. But I would name these men:

Driver	Jack Nicklaus
Fairway woods	Tony Lema
Long irons	Arnold Palmer
Middle irons	Gene Littler
Short irons	Billy Casper
Sand wedge	Julius Boros
Putter	Bob Charles

I saw Nicklaus hit a ball 341 yards at Dallas in the P.G.A. driving contest of 1963. Nicklaus' mechanics are excellent. I believe his tremendous power comes from his legs. He's built more powerfully than Paul Hornung of pro football fame.

At one time, Nicklaus was having trouble with his swing. He was hitting from a closed stance and was locking himself out—not letting his vast power go through the ball. But he made the correction. Most of the time now he hits from a slightly open stance and the ripple of every muscle winds up in the club when the impact is made. That precise timing is what soars the ball over the 300-yard mark.

104   Lema's fairway woods helped him win the British Open, and the World Series of Golf. I played with Lema in the latter tournament,

at Akron. His fairway woods turned the tide on those long, uphill par 4's and the par 5's as well.

Palmer could be chosen for many clubs. I picked him for the long irons because you have to have confidence to play them and Palmer has confidence. Tension is a big factor in the successful execution of the long irons. If tension gets too high, timing is upset. The more the pressure, the better Palmer seems to play.

Few will quarrel with the choice of Littler, Casper and Boros. They are top craftsmen.

But what about a lefthander as the top putter?

Those who saw Charles and Bruce Devlin beat Lema and me in the final of the Columbia Broadcasting System's Golf Classic will not argue. Charles was phenomenal. He has excellent temperament, good concentration and reads the greens remarkably well. Although he doesn't pose officially as such, Charles is a one-man crusade to broadcast to the world that lefthanders, too, can play golf.

Time was when a lefthanded youngster of nine or ten turned out to learn golf, the first thing the conductor of the clinic did was to change him to a righthander. Charles has helped change this trend and stands in powerful defiance of those who discount southpaws. He leads an army of some 400,000 lefthanders, and revolts at the suggestion that righthanded hitters have an advantage. After all, there are as many doglegs right as there are doglegs left.

Johnny Bulla was perhaps the greatest golf switchhitter of all time. He holds course records playing lefthanded and righthanded, which is a significant feat in itself. But, the general belief is, that Bulla could play better lefthanded.

Those of the switching school contend that the great Ben Hogan used to play lefthanded and changed to a righthander. Hitting from the orthodox side, Hogan became one of the all-time greats.

Some converted golfers say they make the switch from left to right without trouble, but they continue to think lefthanded.

I don't know what Charles was thinking when he dropped in those putts against Lema and me but if it's lefthanded thinking, I'd like to have some of it.

Appendix

NICHOLS' AVERAGE
FOR FIRST FIVE YEARS

During his first five years on the professional tour, Bobby Nichols averaged $32,000 a year.

This average is fourth to Arnold Palmer, Jack Nicklaus and Billy Casper, over that period.

Nichols was named most improved player of the year in 1962 by Golf Digest. Also in 1962, he was given the Ben Hogan Award as the golfer who overcame the biggest physical handicap.

In 1964, Nichols was named the middle iron man on Golf magazine's All-American golf team. He was also named the Putter of 1964 by the Golf Writers' of America.

His complete record follows:

	1964		
Finish	*Tournament*	*Score*	*Money*
2d	Los Angeles Open	281	$ 4,000.00
Tied 14th	Bing Crosby National	291	875.00
Tied 50th	Lucky International Open	287	
Tied 33d	Palm Springs Golf Classic	362	346.87
Tied 19th	Phoenix Open	282	787.50
Tied 11th	New Orleans Open	290	1,121.42
Tied 28th	Pensacola Open	284	275.00
Tied 31st	St. Petersburg Open	285	
62d	Doral Open	296	
Tied 11th	Greensboro Open	285	1,250.00
Tied 25th	Masters	291	875.00
Tied 9th	Houston Classic	283	1,569.05
Tied 23d	Texas Open	280	508.33
Tied 19th	Tournament of Champions	291	1,095.00
Tied 48th	Colonial Invitational	300	162.50
Tied 11th	Thunderbird Classic	282	2,000.00
Tied 35th	Buick Open	292	504.30
Tied 14th	U.S. Open	292	900.00
Tied 24th	Cleveland Open	280	816.66
Winner	P.G.A. Championships	271	18,000.00
Tied 23d	Insurance City Open	279	662.50
Tied 5th	St. Paul Open	276	2,560.00
Winner	Carlin World Open	278	35,000.00
Tied 8th	Seattle Open	271	1,450.00
Tied 24th	Mt. View Open	286	475.00

1963

Finish	Tournament	Score	Money
Tied 17th	San Diego Open	278	$ 530.00
Tied 24th	Lucky International	286	575.00
Tied 35th	Phoenix Open	286	150.00
Tied 33d	Tucson Open	287	38.75
Tied 23d	New Orleans Open	293	485.00
Tied 13th	Pensacola Open	279	700.00
11th	St. Petersburg Open	280	850.00
Tied 14th	Doral Open	292	1,125.00
Tied 24th	Masters	295	1,000.00
Tied 10th	Houston Classic	279	1,242.85
Tied 4th	Texas Open	274	1,600.00
Tied 22d	Tournament of Champions	294	1,000.00
Tied 10th	Colonial Invitation	289	1,550.00
10th	Oklahoma City Open	285	1,100.00
Tied 2d	"500" Festival Open	270	3,400.00
Tied 64th	Buick Open	300	
Tied 8th	Thunderbird Classic	281	2,250.00
Tied 14th	U.S. Open	302	900.00
Tied 22d	Hot Springs Open	288	330.00
Tied 23d	P.G.A. Championships	289	775.00
Tied 26th	Western Open	289	425.00
8th	American Golf Classic	285	1,700.00
Tied 14th	Denver Open	284	782.50
Tied 14th	Utah Open	283	900.00
Winner	Seattle Open	272	5,300.00
Tied 14th	Portland Open	278	732.50
Tied 57th	Whitemarsh Open	300	330.00
Tied 4th	Sahara Invitational	278	3,233.34
Tied 23d	Frank Sinatra Open	287	600.00

1962			
Finish	*Tournament*	*Score*	*Money*
Tied 5th	Los Angeles Open	279	$ 1,900.00
Tied 15th	San Diego Open	282	550.00
Tied 54th	Lucky International Open	291	
Tied 32d	Palm Springs Classic	355	164.44
Tied 17th	Phoenix Open	285	608.57
Tied 32d	New Orleans Open	296	126.66
Tied 23d	Baton Rouge Open	286	195.00
Tied 11th	Pensacola Open	278	630.00
Winner	St. Petersburg Open	272	2,800.00
7th	Doral Open	289	1,900.00
Tied 42d	Greensboro Open	297	
Winner	Houston Classic	278	9,000.00
Tied 24th	Texas Open	281	353.34
28th	Tournament of Champions	303	1,000.00
Tied 47th	Colonial Invitational	302	100.00
Tied 6th	Hot Springs Open	279	950.00
Tied 25th	500 Festival Open	276	525.00
Tied 62d	Thunderbird Classic	295	172.50
Tied 3d	U.S. Open	285	5,500.00
5th	Eastern Open	283	1,700.00
52d	Western Open	308	200.00
18th	Motor City Open	279	680.00
6th	P.G.A. Championships	283	2,500.00
Tied 49th	American Golf Classic	298	106.66
Tied 47th	St. Paul Open	287	
Tied 20th	Oklahoma City Open	293	525.00
Tied 19th	Cajun Classic Open	286	256.00
Tied 11th	Mobile Sertoma Open	285	475.00
Tied 15th	Carling Open	284	663.75
Tied 10th	West Palm Beach Open	282	730.00
6th	Haig and Haig Scotch	283	890.00

	1961		
Finish	*Tournament*	*Score*	*Money*
Tied 7th	San Diego Open	277	$ 850.00
Tied 40th	Palm Springs Classic	359	18.33
Tied 50th	Phoenix Open	287	
Tied 24th	Home of the Sun Open	277	182.00
7th	Baton Rouge Open	277	900.00
Tied 21st	Pensacola Open	286	275.00
Tied 64th	St. Petersburg Open	282	
Tied 8th	Sunshine Open	278	950.00
Tied 7th	Azalea Invitational	218	581.00
Tied 21st	Greensboro Open	293	345.00
Tied 44th	Houston Classic	289	150.00
Tied 46th	Texas Open	283	
Tied 37th	Waco Turner Open	296	
Tied 5th	Hot Springs Open	278	962.50
Tied 14th	500 Festival Open	283	1,050.00
Tied 2d	Canadian Open	275	2,233.33
Tied 41st	Milwaukee Open	282	
Tied 6th	Eastern Open	280	1,207.14
Tied 52nd	Insurance City Open	285	
Tied 33d	Carling Open	288	161.43
Tied 43d	American Golf Classic	295	110.00
Tied 20th	Dallas Open	287	470.00
Tied 15th	Denver Open	275	590.00
Tied 56th	Greater Seattle Open	289	
Tied 54th	Portland Open	292	
Tied 14th	Bakersfield Open	283	653.34
Tied 2nd	Ontario Open	277	1,650.00
Tied 10th	Orange County Open	282	655.00
Tied 11th	Beaumont Open	282	610.00
Tied 39th	Cajun Classic Open	287	
Tied 17th	Mobile Sertoma Open	289	218.00
Tied 6th	West Palm Beach Open	281	916.67
Tied 17th	Coral Gables Open	282	358.57

	1960		
Finish	*Tournament*	*Score*	*Money*
Tied 55th	Phoenix Open	291	$
Tied 44th	Texas Open	298	
Tied 37th	Baton Rouge Open	299	
Tied 47th	St. Petersburg Open	299	
Tied 29th	Greater New Orleans Open	286	135.00
Tied 28th	Houston Classic	291	274.28
Tied 19th	Hot Springs Open	284	337.50
Tied 24th	500 Festival Open	278	390.83
Tied 38th	Buick Open	296	130.00
Tied 41st	Western Open	290	115.40
Tied 4th	Eastern Open	277	1,400.00
Tied 27th	Insurance City Open	282	146.67
Tied 23d	St. Paul Open	277	308.75
Tied 15th	Milwaukee Open	281	730.00
Tied 53d	Dallas Open	290	
Tied 42d	Utah Open	278	
Tied 44th	Carling Open	287	
Tied 42nd	Portland Open	287	
Tied 13th	Hesperia Open	287	400.00
Tied 16th	Orange County Open	284	250.00
Tied 42d	Cajun Classic Open	288	
Tied 30th	Mobile Sertoma Open	288	25.00
4th	West Palm Beach Open	287	1,000.00
Tied 27th	Coral Gables Open	286	57.78

INDEX

113